THE UPSCALE OUTDOOR COOKBOOK

*Simple recipes for campers,
backpackers, and short-order
cooks*

by Cari Taylor-Carlson

Serendipity Ink   Milwaukee, Wisconsin

Serendipity Ink
P.O. Box 17163
Milwaukee, WI 53217

Library of Congress Catalog Card Number: 92-80709

First Printing 1992

Illustrations: Lynne Bergschultz
Editing and graphic production: Montgomery Media, Inc.,
                                    Milwaukee, Wisconsin
Cover photos: Mary Eloranta

ISBN 0-9629452-1-8

For my children
Cathy, Linda, Wendy, and Chris
who ate my cooking for 26 years

TABLE
OF CONTENTS

ACKNOWLEDGMENTS

Thanks to hundreds of Tripping Lightly friends who've traveled with me for ten years, and along the way, graciously critiqued my camp food!

Thanks again to the professionals at Montgomery Media, Inc.—I especially appreciate the design talents of Jill Schelbrock and Priya Barnes, and Mary Huntington's editing skills.

A special thank you to Lynne Bergschultz for the illustrations, in particular the playful otters scattered throughout the book. The otter is the only animal that continues to play all through its adult life, and since Tripping Lightly, Inc. promotes playful, serendipitous adventure travel, we've adopted the otter as our corporate symbol.

C.T-C.

"Siestas completed, the pangs of a pinched belly satiated, fur dried and brushed, most otters can think of only one thing to do—play."

C. Madson
High Desert Museum
Bend, Oregon

"Otters are extremely bad at doing nothing . . . they are either asleep or entirely absorbed in play or other activity."

G. Maxwell
High Desert Museum
Bend Oregon

INTRODUCTION

I love to eat! My two favorite activities in order of preference are sharing a candlelit meal with congenial companions on a camping trip, and sleeping under the stars on a sandbar alongside the Green River in Utah's Labyrinth Canyon. Since 1982 when Tripping Lightly, Inc. began, I've taken hundreds of people camping, backpacking, canoeing, and cross-country skiing, and it's been my privilege to prepare meals for them in many spectacular places.

Now it's time to publish a cookbook. Here are the recipes for the meals we serve on Tripping Lightly trips. Simplicity is our goal and healthful, unusual, tasty gourmet meals the end product. You'll find "Fettucine Cantilena" instead of "Hamburger Goulash," and "Eggs Benedict" instead of fried eggs and bacon. In fact, there's not a single hamburger recipe in this cookbook.

Not all of our recipes have hard-to-pronounce names, and not all of them are meant to be cooked over a camp stove. We also cook at home, freeze the meal, and bring it to camp in a cooler. Thus recipes like "Coq au Vin," "Beef Stiffado," and "First Night Chili" are part of the Tripping Lightly recipe collection. We've also found people with busy lives using our recipes. They're "short-order cooks" who find our meals to be quickly and easily prepared and more interesting than hamburgers and frozen fries.

Tripping Lightly guides don't want to slave over camp stoves while the rest of the crew is out playing. Like everyone else, we're there to hike, paddle, read, write, keep a journal, and enjoy lively conversation. This doesn't leave much extra time for cooking chores so I invented, collected, and altered gourmet recipes anyone can follow with minimum effort. Whether I'm in the kitchen at home or on the trail, I won't dirty every pot twice to prepare Boeuf à la Bourguignonne, but I still want it, so I figured out how to do it my way!

Yes, it is possible to hike, canoe, backpack, or cross-country ski, to play all day and still look forward to a feast, quickly prepared and worth waiting for when it's time to eat. At least, that's what the people who travel with Tripping Lightly tell us, and since they pay to be there, they remain our most discriminating critics.

Along with the recipes, I have included quotes from the work of well-known naturalists and outdoor writers because these readings have become a Tripping Lightly tradition. We begin and end each day with a philosophical nugget read aloud. That way if we run out of conversation, we always have thoughts from Edward Abbey or Annie Dillard to gnaw on while we enjoy the scenery.

I hope you enjoy this small collection of simple recipes. Have fun with them, and if you're missing an ingredient, make do. Invent. Experiment. You might even improve on our recipes, and besides, everything really does taste better outdoors!

C.T-C.

BACKPACK
BREAKFASTS

How far is a mile?
Well, you learn that right off.
It's peculiarly different from ten-tenths on the odometer.
It's one thousand seven hundred and sixty
steps on the dead level and if you don't have
anything better to do you can count them.
"One and a half? You're crazy, Jere, we've
been walking for hours!"

It's at least ten and maybe a million times
that on the hills
And no river bed ever does run straight.

"What's this, Frog Creek?
Is that all the further we are?
Look, tomorrow we gotta start earlier."

On The Loose by Jerry and Renny Russell
Sierra Club Books, 1969

Camping has become one of my most beloved pastimes. I
take a fierce delight in swinging a pack onto my back or
into a canoe and heading for the hills or lakes. In my
opinion, camping can be the greatest expression of free
will, personal independence, innate ability, and resource-
fulness possible today in our industrialized urbanized
existence. Regardless of how miserable or how splendid
the circumstances, the sheer experience of camping
seems a total justification for doing it.

Woodswoman by Anne LaBastille
E. P. Dutton, 1976

TALES OF MICE AND BEAR(S)

My heart stopped the morning the bear stole our food bag at Walnut Bottoms back-country site in Smoky Mountains National Park. I stumbled from a deep sleep into morning and found my group giggling at an ambidextrous bear who was pulling our food bag out from under a wooden bridge spanning Big Creek. The night before, after studying the Park Service instructions, we had hung our food properly on their contraption that suspended it three feet below the center of the ten-foot-wide bridge and six feet above Big Creek. We knew our food was safe from predators! Hanging it underneath the bridge wasn't easy, but recent bear activity underscored a need for exceptional precautions.

This time the system didn't work. Somehow, that bear pulled our bag up from beneath the bridge, spread out its contents, and selected his favorite morsels, including our honey and someone's Vaseline. He left us a trail that led to a "dump" where old cartons and wrappers were strewn all over the place. Fortunately, my story has a happy ending because we found almost everything, and he barely touched our food.

That was the first of several incidents at Walnut Bottoms. I've taken groups spring and fall to the Smokies for ten years, and Walnut Bottoms used to be my favorite. I don't go there anymore.

I did return after that first event because I didn't believe a bear could do an acrobatic trick with our food bags twice. We found mice instead. They live under the same bridge, and their mouse condo must be world-famous. Every night during the hiking season, unsuspecting backpackers hang their food under the bridge and those nocturnal critters regularly pirate the food bags. I first learned about the mice when they broke into our food bags, ate their way into the cereal, and left toothmarks on the nuts.

It was April. Big Creek was high and flowing fast. The following night we tightened the bags so the mice couldn't squeeze into them and retired, confident that now our food was safe from predators.

Instead, the mice chewed through the multiple ropes that secured the bags to the bridge. Our food dropped into the river and floated two hundred yards downstream before lodging behind a rock.

The next year the Park Service abandoned their bridge routine and erected a pole where we could hang our food. That worked for a couple of years but we always knew the bears were close-by and we'd often sight one after dark. One night when I felt the ground tremble, I peered out my tent flap and saw a mother and her cub.

Then something serious happened, and I knew I couldn't go back to my favorite site again. One of my group picked up some litter along a trail and stuck it in an outside pocket of her backpack. It's good to pick up trail litter, and we all do it, but the next morning her pack was gone. We followed a trail of debris into the woods for a quarter of a mile before we found her pack. She was lucky. The pack was intact and we saw right away why it had been chosen: next to it lay a chewed Milky Way candy bar wrapper.

Now we camp at an established campground with bear-proof garbage cans and lock our food in the trunk of the car. It's not safe to backpack where the bears are so aggressive, and more importantly, where they've lost their instinctive fear of us.

SUPER PANCAKES WITH RED-HOT COMPOTE

This is a favorite breakfast on our backpacking trips. The compote's pink sauce has a good cinnamon-candy flavor.

2   cups Bisquick or any other pancake mix

$\frac{1}{4}$ cup instant dry milk

1   T. dry egg replacer

1   cup water

$1\frac{1}{2}$ cups chopped dry apples

$\frac{1}{2}$ cup cinnamon imperials (red-hots)

2   cups water

        raisins, walnuts and pecans (optional)

At home: Mix together pancake mix, dry milk, and dry egg replacer, and store in a plastic bag. In a separate bag, combine apples, red-hots, and optional nuts and raisins.

At camp: Add 2 cups water to the apple mix, bring to a boil in a covered pot, simmer for 5 minutes and let sit while you cook the pancakes. The apples will absorb about half the water and they'll turn rosy pink. Add additional water as needed to stretch the sauce. Add 1 cup water to the pancake mix and fry the pancakes in margarine. Serve with compote in place of syrup.

Serves 4.

CORNBREAD WITH MUSHROOM SAUCE

It's always a surprise how good this tastes on a leisurely morning. Most of us don't eat mushroom sauce for breakfast at home, but after a few days in the woods, this is a special treat.

2	T. margarine
1	8 $\frac{1}{2}$-oz. box Jiffy cornbread mix
$\frac{1}{2}$	cup parmesan cheese
$\frac{1}{3}$	cup water
1	T. dry egg replacer
2	T. instant dry milk
1	1.9-oz. package mushroom soup mix
$\frac{1}{2}$	cup instant dry milk
2	cups water

At home: Combine the cornbread mix, parmesan cheese, dry egg replacer, and 2 T. dry milk in one bag, and the soup mix and $\frac{1}{2}$ cup dry milk in another bag.

At camp: Heat margarine in a fry pan with a lid. Combine the cornbread ingredients with $\frac{1}{3}$ cup water and spread evenly in the fry pan. Cover and cook over low heat for 15 minutes. Heat 2 cups water and add the soup/sauce mix. Cook over low heat until thickened. Spoon sauce over bread.

Serves 4-6.

CORNMEAL MUSH

1   cup cornmeal

1   cup dried apples, chopped

$4\frac{1}{2}$ cups water

salt to taste

At home: Combine all ingredients and bag.

At camp: In a saucepan, bring the water to a boil. Gradually add the cornmeal/apple mix , stirring constantly. Cover and simmer for 15 minutes. Serve with margarine and brown sugar.

Serves 4.

SPECIAL GRANOLA CEREAL

There's satisfaction in making your own cereal. Keep this mix in the refrigerator and it will last indefinitely.

1   cup filberts (hazelnuts)

1   cup toasted and chopped almonds

3   cups quick oatmeal

1   cup wheat germ

1   cup chopped apricots

1   cup raisins

1   cup instant dry milk

1   T. cinnamon

1   t. nutmeg

At home: Combine all ingredients.

At camp: Cook five minutes, using one part cereal to one part water. Serve with margarine and brown sugar.

Serves 4-6.

YUMMY CEREAL

2 cups oatmeal

1 cup wheat germ

1 cup whole wheat flour

1½ cups brown sugar

1 cup broken walnuts

1 t. vanilla

1 cup vegetable oil

At home: Heat oil in a large skillet and add the rest of the ingredients. Stir carefully to coat the grains with oil, and cook slowly on medium heat until it darkens and begins to stick together. It will keep for 2 months in the refrigerator.

At camp: Eat it cold, or add water and heat it briefly.

Serves 4-6

COLD MORNING WHEAT CEREAL

You can fix this without adding the nuts and fruits, but why? Experiment with a variety of both.

1 cup bulgur

¼ cup instant dry milk

⅓ cup each of raisins, nuts, and dry chopped apples

2-3 cups water

brown sugar

margarine

cinnamon

At home: Combine bulgur, dry milk, raisins, nuts, and apples.

At camp: Add dry ingredients to 2 cups water and simmer for 10 minutes. Add more water if necessary. Remove from heat and let stand for 5 minutes before serving with margarine, brown sugar, and cinnamon.

Serves 4.

OATS AND GROATS

Be sure to cook it until the groats are tender.

$\frac{1}{2}$ cup rolled oats (not instant)

$\frac{1}{2}$ cup buckwheat groats

$\frac{1}{2}$ cup chopped dried apricots

$\frac{1}{2}$ cup chopped pecans

2 $\frac{1}{2}$ cups water

At home: Combine the first four ingredients.

At camp: Add ingredients to the water. Simmer for 15 minutes and serve with margarine, brown sugar, and cinnamon.

Serves 4.

BANANA-PECAN PANCAKES

Improve this one with fresh bananas!

2	cups Bisquick or any other pancake mix
1/4	cup instant dry milk
1	T. dry egg replacer
1	cup chopped pecans
1/2	cup dried bananas
1	cup water (approximate)

At home: Combine the pancake mix, dry egg replacer, dry milk, pecans and dried bananas.

At camp: Add water to mix, let stand for 10 minutes, then fry in margarine. Serve with brown sugar syrup.

Serves 4.

BREAKFAST CREAM OF COUSCOUS

Couscous for breakfast tastes like the Cream of Wheat we ate back in the '50s.

2 cups water

2 T. margarine

1 cup couscous

$\frac{1}{4}$ cup walnuts

$\frac{1}{4}$ cup chopped dried apricots

3 T. brown sugar

1 t. cinnamon

2 T. instant dry milk

At home: Combine couscous, nuts, fruit, sugar, cinnamon, and dry milk.

At camp: Bring water and margarine to a boil. Add dry mix and simmer for 5 minutes. Let sit for another 5 minutes and serve.

Serves 4.

APPLE PANCAKES

Apples are heavy, but it's well worth the extra weight to enjoy these pancakes in the wilderness.

1   large apple, cut into small slices

2   cups Bisquick or any pancake mix

¼   cup instant dry milk

1   T. dry egg replacer

1   T. brown or white sugar

1   t. cinnamon.

1   cup water

At home: Combine Bisquick or pancake mix, dry milk, dry egg replacer, sugar, and cinnamon.

At camp: Add the apple and the water to the dry mix and cook in margarine. Serve with brown sugar syrup, or if you serve it at an established camp, top with vanilla yogurt and applesauce.

Serves 4.

HASH BROWN POTATOES WITH CHEESE

If you're in a hurry, the potatoes will rehydrate faster if they simmer instead of sit.

 1   6-oz. box dry hash brown potatoes

 ½   cup grated cheese

 water

 2   T. margarine

 salt and pepper to taste

At home: Pack the potatoes and cheese separately. Parmesan cheese works well; otherwise, grate the cheese at camp.

At camp: Rehydrate potatoes by bringing 3 cups of water to a simmer. Add hash browns, cover tightly, remove from heat and allow to sit for 15 minutes. Drain, then saute the potatoes in 2 T. margarine until browned. Stir in cheese, remove from heat, and eat when the cheese is melted.

Serves 2.

HASH BROWN FRITTERS

Similar to the preceding recipe but served with sweet syrup in place of melted cheese.

1   6-oz. box dry hash brown potatoes

3   T. instant dry milk

2   t. flour

2   T. dry egg replacer

salt to taste

1   small onion, sliced

6   T. water

At home: Put the potatoes in one plastic bag and the dry ingredients in another. Put both in a third bag along with the onion.

At camp: Bring the potatoes to a simmer in 3 cups water, cover tightly, and let sit for 15 minutes to rehydrate. In a bowl, mix the dry ingredients, the drained potatoes, and 6 T. water. Saute the onion in 2 T. margarine, add the potato mix and saute for 3-4 minutes on each side. Serve with brown sugar syrup.

Serves 3-4.

GINGERBREAD PANCAKES

This one is easy. Buy a gingerbread cake and cookie mix and combine with Bisquick for an unusual pancake treat.

1   cup Bisquick

1   cup gingerbread cake and cookie mix

¼   cup instant dry milk

1   T. dry egg replacer

¾   cup water (approximate)

raisins (optional)

At home: Combine Bisquick, gingerbread mix, dry milk, dry egg replacer, and optional raisins.

At camp: Add ¾ cup water to the dry mix and fry in margarine. Serve with brown sugar syrup.

Serves 4.

LEMON SAUCE

Serve on gingerbread pancakes for a treat.

$\frac{1}{2}$ cup sugar

1   cup water

1   T. margarine

1   oz. lemon juice (half a film container)

1   T. cornstarch

At home: Combine sugar and cornstarch.

At camp: Combine sugar, cornstarch, water, and lemon juice. Cook slowly until thick. Add margarine and stir.

BROWN SUGAR SYRUP

$\frac{1}{2}$ cup brown sugar

$\frac{1}{2}$ cup water

2   T. margarine

$\frac{1}{2}$ t. cinnamon

$\frac{1}{4}$ t. nutmeg

vanilla (optional)

Simmer sugar, water, and spices for 1 minute. Add margarine and vanilla and serve over pancakes.

CAMPGROUND BREAKFASTS

(continued on next page)

(Campground Breakfasts continued)

April 26. Mother is putting my new secondhand clothes in order. She prays now, she says, that I may learn in my own life and away from home and friends what the heart is and what it feels. Amen. So be it. Welcome, O life! I go to encounter for the millionth time the reality of experience and to forge in the smithy of my soul the uncreated conscience of my race.

A Portrait of the Artist as a Young Man by James Joyce
The Viking Press Inc., 1916

At home, when I meet my friends in those cubby-holed hours, time is so precious we feel we must cram every available instant with conversation. We cannot afford the luxury of silence. Here on the island I find I can sit with a friend without talking, sharing the day's last sliver of pale green light on the horizon, or the whorls in a small white shell, or the dark scar left in a dazzling night sky by a shooting star. Then communication becomes communication and one is nourished as one never is by words.

Gift from the Sea by Anne Morrow Lindbergh
Signet Books, 1955

O world, I cannot hold thee close enough!
Thy winds, thy wide grey skies!
Thy mists, that roll and rise!
Thy woods, this autumn day, that ache and sag
And all but cry with colour! That gaunt crag
To crush! To lift the lean of that black bluff!
World! world, I cannot get thee close enough.

Long have I known a glory in it all,
But never knew I this;
Here such a passion is
As stretcheth me apart — Lord, I do fear
Thou'st made the world too beautiful this year;
My soul is all but out of me — let fall
No burning leaf; prithee, let no bird call.

Poems Selected for Young People by Edna St. Vincent Millay
Harper and Row, 1917

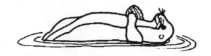

About Food

Warning — air travel may be hazardous to cucumbers and bananas. Once when I was packing the food, adding cucumbers to our trail lunches and fresh bananas to the banana-pecan pancakes sounded like a great idea. The cukes and bananas were stored carefully in the middle of the "food duffel" going to Jackson, Wyoming for a week-long trip to Grand Teton National Park.

There are grocery stores in Jackson, of course, but I thought it was easier to bring everything from home and avoid wasting time shopping when I could be on the trail. Someone has to make the grocery store runs and it's always the guide(s), so we plan ahead, taking massive quantities of food on the airplane. We use oversize duffel bags, and it's not unusual to pack one hundred pounds of food and fly it from Wisconsin to Wyoming.

On a wilderness trip, particularly a backpacking trip, our approximate rule of thumb is one pound of food per person per day so the airline food bags for backpacking trips stay at a reasonable weight. We know that when it's time to set off down the trail, we have to carry those same food bags on our backs. On trips where we stay at established campgrounds, we eat whatever we're willing to cook, and food weight has no relevance. The airlines limit duffel bags to seventy pounds each; my personal limit depends on whether I can drag the food duffel out my door, down the steps, and lift it into the car. If I can, then I know the weight doesn't exceed seventy pounds. It was one of those heavy ones that liquified the cucumber and mangled the bananas. Since those early learning experiences, I don't fly anything that won't stand up to the rigors of luggage handlers and air travel. Perhaps we should have included the mashed bananas in the banana-pecan pancakes, but because they had escaped their peels and covered the inside of the food bag with banana slime, we trashed the mess.

When I pack food for backpacking, I take a different approach. Due to weight restrictions, I begin by removing the packaging from the grocery store items. I'll never get used to the excessive amount of stuff that surrounds each item! I cut, rip, tear, and discard plastic, cardboard, and foam, and watch garbage bag after garbage bag overflow with this surplus trash.

Each meal is packaged individually in plastic ziplock bags or baggies, then double-bagged. Between the two bags, I write specific instructions for the trail cook. It may appear superfluous to write down the exact amount of water to add to the breakfast cereal after twenty years, but I still do it every time because I'm likely to forget when I cook a different breakfast every day.

We have two reasons for double-bagging. First, the system provides a place for instructions. Equally important, two bags mean less food smell and that guarantees fewer unwelcome guests. We want to keep our food safe from all vandalizing critters, and the best way to do that is to extinguish food smells. Years ago a bear ripped open one of our food bags at Pictured Rocks National Lakeshore, and we determined that since the food was stored and hung in an ordinary stuff sack, the bear's nose had led it straight to our cache. Now we store and hang food in two heavy-duty garbage bags, and since we switched, we have a perfect record.

In grizzly country, even minor carelessness is never acceptable. Back in the late '70s, six of us went into the Scapegoat Wilderness in Montana to backpack for twelve days. We sounded like Santa's reindeer as we walked down the trail with our bear insurance tied on our hiking boots. After the first day we knew we could take off our bells because conversation won't lag among six women, and our chatter kept the bears away just as effectively as the jingling "bear bells."

At night we arranged camp in an equilateral triangle. We pitched the tents at one point, another served as the kitchen, and we hung our food at the third point. We hung up our cooking clothes, we washed carefully after meals, and we took every precaution to keep food odor out of the tents. One can't be too careful in griz country. It's all the same. Keeping bears at bay and flying cucumbers and bananas from Milwaukee, Wisconsin to Jackson, Wyoming. With common sense and a little bit of know-how, we can take care of ourselves and our belongings wherever we go.

Huevos Rancheros

Don't plan this breakfast on a quick get-away day, but wait for a mellow morning when everyone's asleep and you can surprise them with this tasty southwestern breakfast.

2 eggs per person

1 15-oz. can of refried beans

flour tortillas

grated cheddar cheese

sour cream

1 jar of salsa or picante sauce

1 onion (optional)

1 green pepper (optional)

1 T. vegetable oil

Chop the (optional) onion and green pepper and saute them in the oil. Add the refried beans and heat gently. If you omit the onion and pepper, still use oil in the pan to heat the beans so they won't glue themselves to the bottom of the skillet. Scramble 2 eggs per person.

Layer on individual plates:
> bean mix
> eggs
> grated cheddar cheese
> 1 T. sour cream
> 1 T. salsa

Scoop it all up with a fork and a flour tortilla. Serves as many as you wish, depending on the number of eggs.

Eggs McBagel

Somewhat like McDonald's famous recipe; however, the eggs won't be perfectly round to match the bagels.

4	bagels
1/2	lb. boiled ham
4	eggs
4	slices american or cheddar cheese
1	T. butter or margarine

Fry the eggs, and when each one is almost done, lay a slice of cheese on top to melt. Toast the bagels and make a sandwich with the fried egg and cheese, ham, and bagel.

Serves 4.

Spiced Bananas

Don't overcook the bananas, or they'll turn slimy.

4	bananas
1	T. butter or margarine
1/4	cup water
2	T. brown sugar
1/2	t. cinnamon

Combine butter or margarine, water, sugar, and cinnamon. Bring to a simmer, add the bananas, cover, and simmer for 4 minutes. Turn them once.

Serves 4.

Seafood Hollandaise Surprise

8   eggs

4   slices whole grain bread, toasted

2   sliced tomatoes

1   1.9-oz. package hollandaise sauce mix

1   cup milk

1   stick margarine

juice of ½ to 1 whole lemon (to taste)

1   small can crabmeat

1   small can shrimp

Make the hollandaise sauce according to the package directions. Add lemon juice, shrimp, and crab and keep the mixture warm. Toast the bread, slice the tomatoes, and scramble the eggs. Layer toast, tomatoes, eggs, and sauce.

Serves 4.

CURRIED CHEESY HAM AND EGGS

1    $10\,^3/_4$-oz. can of condensed cheddar cheese soup

1   chopped tomato

1   4-oz. can of sliced mushrooms, drained

1   cup diced cooked ham

1   t. curry powder

$1/_4$ t. garlic salt

8   eggs (2 per person)

4   english muffins

Heat soup, tomato, mushrooms, ham, garlic salt, and curry. Scramble the eggs and toast the muffins. Divide the eggs into four portions. Serve the eggs on the toasted muffins and spoon the ham and cheese sauce over the eggs. This recipe can be altered by using a different kind of toasted bread or by preparing the eggs in a different way (i.e., frying, poaching).

Serves 4.

CORNED BEEF AND BROWN RICE

1	cup instant brown rice
1	cup water
1	onion, chopped
2	T. butter or margarine
1	12-oz. can corned beef, flaked
4	eggs
2	T. mustard

Bring the cup of water to a boil and add the rice. Simmer for one minute, cover tightly, and set aside for 10-15 minutes. Saute the onion in margarine. Combine the cooked rice, corned beef, and mustard and add to the pan with the sauteed onions. Make four pockets in the mixture and drop an egg into each one. Cover the pan and cook over low heat until the eggs are done to taste (10-20 minutes). You can also fry the eggs separately and serve on top of the corned beef mixture. Good with or without catsup.

Serves 4.

POLENTA AND SAUSAGE

This combination makes a good, filling breakfast.

1 cup cornmeal

3½ cups water

2 T. butter or margarine

1 t. salt

8 smoked sausages (pre-cooked and cut into chunks)

½ cup parmesan cheese

maple syrup

Bring the water to a boil. Pour in the cornmeal slowly, stirring constantly. Cook on low heat, stirring occasionally, for 15 to 20 minutes, or until the polenta is stiff. Stir in the butter or margarine, cheese and sausages, and heat together before serving with plenty of maple syrup. Change the flavor by adding cheddar and/or monterey jack cheeses.

Serves 4.

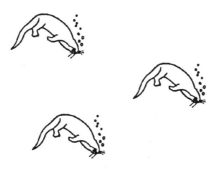

DELUXE CHIPPED BEEF

This recipe comes from the Peoria, Illinois Junior League Cookbook, which was published in the early 1960s B.C. (Before Cholesterol).

1	5-oz. package chipped beef, cut in strips
2	T. butter or margarine
1	onion, chopped
3	T. flour
1	cup milk
1	cup sour cream
1	cup cheddar cheese, grated
1	sliced tomato
4	english muffins

Saute the beef and onion in butter or margarine. Add flour and stir until well mixed. Slowly add milk, stirring constantly until the sauce thickens. Add sour cream, cheddar cheese, and serve over toasted english muffins and sliced tomato.

Serves 4.

Cari's Eggs

It's fun to experiment with eggs, and here's a winner!

4	english muffins
2	T. butter or margarine
2	green onions or shallots, chopped
8	oz. provolone cheese, grated
$\frac{1}{2}$	cup black olives, pitted and sliced
8	eggs, beaten

salt and pepper to taste

Heat butter or margarine in a skillet and saute the onions. Beat the eggs, and add cheese, olives, salt and pepper. Cook in skillet with onions over low heat until the eggs are set. Serve over toasted english muffins or bagels.

Serves 4.

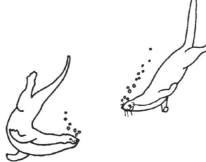

Eggs Foo Yung

1   medium-sized onion, chopped

2   T. butter or margarine

1   15-oz. can of bean sprouts, well-drained

8   eggs, beaten

soy sauce

Saute chopped onion in butter or margarine. Mix the bean sprouts with the eggs and scramble with onions until eggs are firm. Serve with soy sauce.

Serves 4.

HOPPLE POPPLE

We used to eat this often for dinner at home. During my vegetarian years, I would leave out the salami and call it simply "Eggs and Potatoes."

8   eggs

2   T. water

3   medium-sized potatoes, diced

1   large onion, chopped

¼   lb. salami, cut into chunks

3   T. butter or margarine

sour cream

salt and pepper to taste

Saute the onions and potatoes in butter or margarine. Cover and fry over low heat until the potatoes are cooked. Loosen the potatoes occasionally and stir to brown them. Beat the eggs, and add the water, salt and pepper, and salami. Scramble with the eggs and potatoes. Serve with a spoonful of sour cream.

Serves 4.

Jesse's Boozled Eggs

"Boozled" may not be an official cooking term, but my guide Mary Eloranta's daughter Jesse "boozled" them at Girl Scout Camp and so do we.

8	eggs
1/2	cup milk
	salt and pepper to taste
1/4	t. nutmeg
4	bagels, split
1/2	lb. boiled ham
1	cup grated swiss cheese
2	T. butter or margarine

Beat eggs, add milk, nutmeg, salt and pepper, and mix well. Heat butter or margarine and "boozle" the eggs. To "boozle," stir constantly until cooked through. They will not look like scrambled eggs, but will have the consistency of very small curd cottage cheese. Toast the bagels, and layer the ham, "boozled" eggs, and grated cheese on top of them.

Serves 4.

Chili Eggs

8 eggs

½ cup milk

½ T. chili powder

salt and pepper to taste

4 oz. cream cheese, sliced in cubes

1 4 oz. can of chopped green chilis

sour cream

salsa, medium hot

flour tortillas

grated cheddar cheese

Beat the eggs with milk and spices. Add cream cheese and green chilis. Scramble and serve with sour cream, salsa, and cheese. Scoop it all up with a warm flour tortilla.

Serves 4.

DESCHUTES RIVER FRENCH TOAST

I first ate this on the Deschutes River in central Oregon on a rafting trip run by Oregon River Experiences. It's become a popular Tripping Lightly breakfast.

3   pieces of bread per person

1   egg per person (beaten)

vanilla to taste

milk (1 T. per egg)

$\frac{1}{4}$ t. cinnamon for every four servings

1   14-oz. can of blueberries, or a 21-oz can of cherry, apple, or blueberry pie filling

$\frac{1}{2}$ cup vanilla yogurt per person

butter or margarine

Mix eggs, vanilla, cinnamon, and milk. Dip bread in mixture and fry in butter or margarine until golden brown. Serve with a spoonful of yogurt and fruit. A combination of fresh lemon juice and powdered sugar also makes a delicious topping.

EGGS BENEDICT

We used to do "veggie" eggs benedict, using onions, mushrooms, and peppers during the green and brown years of Tripping Lightly cuisine, but it's much better with ham.

4	english muffins
1	1.9-oz. package of hollandaise sauce mix
$1/_2$	lb. thinly sliced boiled ham
8	eggs
1	cup dry milk
1	stick butter or margarine
	juice of 1 lemon

Split and toast the muffins. Make the hollandaise sauce according to the package directions, and add lemon juice. Divide the ham among the 8 muffin halves. Poach, fry, or scramble the eggs. Layer the ham and eggs on the muffin halves and spoon the sauce over the top.

Serves 4.

CAMPER'S CORNED BEEF HASH

A Carlson family favorite.

1	onion, chopped
1	green pepper, chopped
4	T. butter or margarine
1	6-oz. box hash brown potatoes
1	12-oz. can corned beef, shredded

grated cheese (optional)

catsup (optional)

Saute onion and pepper in butter or margarine. Rehydrate potatoes by bringing 3 cups of water to a simmer, adding hash browns and covering tightly. Remove from heat and let stand for 10 minutes before draining and combining them with the corned beef. Add to the onion and peppers and fry over medium heat, stirring often, until the mixture is crusty. If it sticks to the pan, add more butter or margarine. Serve with optional cheese and catsup.

Serves 3-4.

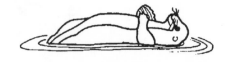

Huevos, Puerto Escondito

1   5-oz. package chipped beef, sliced

3   T. butter or margarine

1   cup parmesan cheese

1   15 ½-oz. can of stewed tomatoes

½   T. chili powder

8   eggs, beaten

flour tortillas

sour cream

cheddar cheese

Saute chipped beef in butter or margarine. Add tomatoes, cheese, and chili powder. Simmer for 5 minutes. Add beaten eggs, mix well, and cook over low heat until eggs are firm. Serve on warm tortillas with the sour cream and grated cheese.

Serves 4.

Greek Eggs and Cheese

2   T. olive oil

4   slices provolone cheese

4   eggs

salt and pepper

juice of 1 lemon

4   slices toast, bagel, or english muffin

Warm olive oil in skillet. Place slices of cheese in the oil, and just as the cheese begins to soften, break eggs over the cheese, taking care not to break the yolk. Sprinkle with salt and pepper. Cover the skillet and cook the eggs over low heat. It takes about 10 minutes. As soon as the yolks are almost firm, squeeze lemon juice over the eggs and lift on to toast with a spatula. Don't leave any juice in the pan. It's delicious when it soaks into the toast.

Serves 2.

FANCY HERBED EGGS

This breakfast won't come out of the pan looking like the photos on the lovely cover of Gourmet *magazine, but it tastes as if it belongs there.*

8   eggs

1   large onion

2   T. butter or margarine

1   15 ½-oz. can of stewed tomatoes

salt and pepper to taste

¼   t. baking soda

1   T. flour

1   t. tarragon

1   cup grated cheddar cheese

sour cream

Beat eggs well with flour. Saute onion in butter or margarine. Add stewed tomatoes and salt and pepper. Bring to a simmer and add the baking soda. Stir in eggs, and cook over low heat until thick and the eggs are set. Serve on toast with grated cheese and sour cream.

Serves 4.

PINEAPPLE SAUCE

Another good topping for gingerbread pancakes. Because the pineapple comes in a can, it is better to prepare this recipe at an established campground.

1	8-oz. can of crushed pineapple (do not drain)
3/4	cup cold water
1/4	cup sugar
1	T. cornstarch
1/2	stick margarine

Combine water, sugar, and cornstarch and cook slowly until thick. Add the margarine and pineapple, and serve at once.

CINNAMON CANNED PEACHES

Cut up a can of peaches, add cinnamon and nutmeg, heat gently and serve over gingerbread or banana-pecan pancakes.

LUNCH

Simplicity in all things is the secret of the wilderness and one of its most valuable lessons. It is what we leave behind that is important. I think the matter of simplicity goes further than just food, equipment, and unnecessary gadgets; it goes into the matter of thoughts and objectives as well. When in the wilds, we must not carry our problems with us or the joy is lost.

Reflections from the North Country by Sigurd F. Olson
Alfred A. Knopf Inc.,1976

I am bound to praise the simple life, because I have lived it and found it good. When I depart from it, evil results follow. I love a small house, plain clothes, simple living. Many persons know the luxury of a skin bath—a plunge in the pool or the wave unhampered by clothing. This is the simple life—direct and immediate contact with things, life with the false wrappings torn away—the fine house, the fine equipage, the expensive habits, all cut off. How free one feels, how good the elements taste, how close one gets to them, how they fit one's body and one's soul! To see the fire that warms you; to see the spring where the water bubbles up that slakes your thirst, and to dip your pail into it; to see the beams that are the stay of your four walls, and the timbers that uphold the roof that shelters you; to be in direct and personal contact with the sources of your material life; to want no extras, no shields; to find the universal elements enough; to find the air and the water exhilarating; to be refreshed by a morning walk or an evening saunter; to find a quest of wild berries more satisfying than a gift of tropic fruit; to be thrilled by the stars at night; to be elated over a bird's nest, or over a wildflower in spring—these are some of the rewards of the simple life.

John Burroughs, reprinted in *The Earth Speaks*,
edited by Steve Van Matre and Bill Weiler.
Acclimatization Experiences Institute, 1983

THE EXPLODING BEAN DIP

Once I tried to impress a group with an unusual, creative, diverse lunch. Season after season we hear kudos from participants on our Tripping Lightly adventures, and once in a while, mingled with the praise, we find comments about the trail lunches.

When it comes to food, it's unreasonable to try to please everyone all the time, but it's our belief we should please most of them most of the time. Breakfasts and dinners are easy, but lunch—now there's the problem meal!

On a canoe trip we score one hundred percent. When we tip over a canoe on shore, spread a tablecloth, and set out chips, dips, chopped veggies, whole-grain breads, sandwich makings, fresh fruit, cold cider, soda, and for dessert, something rich and sweet we made at home, everyone digs in with gusto.

We bring coolers and there's plenty of canoe space for bags of fresh food. A trail lunch presents a different set of problems. It should be compact, of a reasonable weight, and something we can eat on the ground. It must have visual appeal, and if it needs refrigeration, forget it. We always ask our groups, "How can we improve the trail lunch?" and the standard response is and always has been "diversify."

In 1991, on the Yellowstone-Teton cross-country ski trip, I made ten individual lunches that came from a composite suggestion bank that dated back to Tripping Lightly's early days. This was going to be the ultimate lunch everyone would remember. The mountains, the elk, the geyser basin, the bison, the blizzard conditions, fantastic snow in Yellowstone, and the breathtaking scenery at the canyon all would pale in comparison to "the lunch."

I planned for weeks. On a trip like this, breakfasts and

dinners are lodge meals and the biggest decision anyone has to make is whether to order eggs benedict for breakfast, or poached salmon with dill or filet mignon with bearnaise sauce for dinner. A meal sandwiched between eggs en cocotte and broiled tournedos with potatoes Anna needs a special quality to make it memorable. This could not be an ordinary, humble trail lunch.

I made list after list and revision after revision until I found the perfect combination of carbohydrate, protein, fruit, and sugar. In ten separate bags, I packed dry apricots, dry apples, five kinds of bread (pita, pumpernickel, tortillas, cocktail rye, and a bagel), three spreads (bean dip, cream cheese with green olives and walnuts, and a fancy cheddar cheese mix), one-half pound of plain muenster cheese, one-quarter pound crunchy peanut butter, one-half pound of salami, a bag of trail mix embellished with candy, and two plastic knives to cut and spread. Now, that's lunch!

Was it memorable? Yes, it certainly was, but for the wrong reason. We had a minor problem because our indoor accommodations had no refrigeration and the outdoor temperature hovered around zero. Most of the group was too polite to tell me about their lunches and since my bag of food remained normal, I thought lunch was perfect at last! It was a scene straight from "The Emperor's New Clothes"—the one in which he walks naked in the parade, and everyone applauds his tailor and his good taste.

While I was congratulating myself, the others were snickering because their bean dip was producing gas, their cream cheese had grown a lovely green intricate net of mold, and their pita bread had developed brown spots. We were close to the end of the trip before someone finally told me. We had a good belly-laugh over my "diverse" lunch as we trashed the expanding beans, the webbed green cheese, and the greenish-brown spotted pita.

I still blush when someone kids me about the disastrous super lunch, and that's the last time I attempted diversity on the trail. Now we do a standard lunch. People who travel with Tripping Lightly can expect cheese spread, peanut butter, hard bread, sesame sticks, dried fruit, and the usual high energy trail mix combined with assorted candy. Weather permitting, we might toss in a group cucumber. It's not fancy, but we know that after several days nothing will grow on it, and when we describe gassy beans and fuzzy green cheese, no one complains!

BACKPACKER'S TRAIL LUNCH

We supply a basic lunch when we take people on hiking and canoe camping trips. We plan no-frill lunches to provide enough calories and to maintain interest in the daily noon trail meal. Each person carries his or her own lunch, and is responsible for portioning out the food for the duration of the trip.

8   oz. durable bread:
    (bagels, flour tortillas, rye, pumpernickel,
    hard crackers)

8   oz. processed cheese spread

6   oz. chunky peanut butter

4   oz. dry fruit (especially apples)

6   oz. sesame sticks (Pepperidge Farm et al)

This lunch weighs approximately 2 pounds and will supply an average hiker with a noontime meal for 5-7 days.

REFRIED TORTILLA SPREAD

1   16-oz. can of refried beans

1   small red onion, chopped

1   cup mayonnaise

Combine and serve in flour tortillas with salsa and sour cream.

Serves 8.

A Sweet Sandwich

8   oz. cream cheese

1   cup dry fruit and nuts, chopped (or a commercial trail mix)

2   T. honey

2   T. lemon juice

Mix everything together and put in pita bread.

Serves 6.

Almond-Chutney Sandwich Spread

8   oz. cream cheese

$\frac{1}{2}$ cup sour cream

2   green onions, sliced

$\frac{1}{2}$ cup toasted almonds, chopped

2   t. curry powder

$\frac{1}{2}$ cup finely diced chutney

Soften the cream cheese and mix all ingredients together. Spread on a french baguette or croissant.

Serves 4.

LUNCHTIME BURRITO

1 16-oz. can refried beans

½ lb. cheddar cheese, sliced or grated

1 red onion, sliced thin

1 avocado, sliced

2 tomatoes, sliced

2 cups shredded lettuce or alfalfa sprouts

salsa

sour cream

flour tortillas

Set everything out buffet style and let each person roll his or her own burrito combo inside a flour tortilla. Serve with plenty of napkins, because when you do it right, you'll have sour cream and salsa dripping off your chin.

Serves 8.

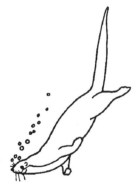

ELEVEN UNUSUAL SANDWICHES

Some of these sandwich ideas come from D. B. Kaplan's Delicatessen in Water Tower Place on Michigan Avenue in Chicago. The rest are inventions that resulted from slapping together items found in my refrigerator.

1. Salami, provolone cheese, thinly sliced red onion, tomato, and mustard on french bread.

2. Roast beef, turkey, muenster cheese, shredded lettuce, thinly sliced red onion, and russian dressing on rye bread.

3. Baked ham, salami, cheddar cheese, shredded lettuce, sliced tomatoes and russian dressing on whole-wheat bread.

4. Turkey, cream cheese, prosciutto ham, and mustard on pumpernickel bread.

5. Roast beef, bacon, muenster cheese, shredded lettuce, and russian dressing on rye bread.

6. Liver sausage, roast beef, swiss cheese, shredded lettuce, and russian dressing on pumpernickel bread.

7. Prosciutto ham, provolone cheese, sliced red onion, horseradish and mustard on french bread.

8. Turkey, shredded lettuce, and whole cranberry sauce on french bread.

9. Canadian bacon, cheddar cheese, and coleslaw on a kaiser roll.

10. Liver sausage, bacon, pickle relish, lettuce, sliced tomato, and mayonnaise on rye bread.

11. Canadian bacon, hickory smoked bacon, american cheese, shredded lettuce, sliced tomato, and mayonnaise on whole-wheat bread.

CHIPPED BEEF SANDWICH

$\frac{1}{2}$ cup sour cream

8   oz. cream cheese

1   5-oz. package chipped beef, sliced

1   t. dill seeds

2   ribs celery, sliced

sliced tomatoes

Soften the cream cheese, and mix with chipped beef, dill seeds, and celery. Serve on pumpernickel bread with sliced tomatoes.

Serves 4.

AVOCADO AND BACON SPREAD

1   avocado, sliced

$\frac{1}{3}$ lb. muenster cheese, sliced

8   oz. bacon, fried crisp

alfalfa sprouts

Combine in pita bread or make a sandwich with any whole grain bread.

Serves 4.

CHICKEN IN CREAM CHEESE

8   oz. cream cheese

2   5-oz. cans of chicken, chopped (or poach a chicken breast instead)

1   small red onion, chopped

1   green pepper, diced

3   celery ribs, sliced

$\frac{1}{2}$ cup mayonnaise

Mix and spread on rye bread.

Serves 6-8.

FANCY CHEESE SPREAD

1   lb. cheddar cheese, grated

1   bunch green onions, sliced

2   celery ribs, sliced

$\frac{1}{2}$ cup black olives, sliced

1   cup mayonnaise

Combine all ingredients and serve in pita bread with sweet pickle relish, or on whole wheat bread with bread-and-butter pickles.

Serves 6-8.

CHEESE AND VEGGIE SPREAD

This is the classic Tripping Lightly "riverbank" lunch. We turn over a canoe, spread the tablecloth, and set out the food. We also include chips, cut-up veggies, dip, fresh fruit, and a dessert.

$\frac{1}{2}$ lb. swiss cheese, sliced

$\frac{1}{2}$ lb. cheddar cheese, sliced

$\frac{1}{2}$ lb. monterey jack cheese, sliced

avocado, sliced

alfalfa sprouts

shredded lettuce

sliced tomato

sliced red onion

sliced green pepper

mayonnaise

fancy mustard(s)

assorted whole grain breads

pita bread, bagels, or flour tortillas

Set it all out buffet style.

Serves 8-10.

POWER PEANUT BUTTER

1½   cups peanut butter

½   cup honey

1   stick margarine

1   cup powdered milk

1   cup sunflower seeds

1   cup raisins

Melt margarine and mix everything together.

Serves many.

DELUXE SHRIMP SPREAD

8   oz. cream cheese

2   4-oz. cans shrimp, drained

½   cup sour cream

1   bunch green onions, sliced

2   celery ribs, chopped

½   green pepper, diced

Soften the cream cheese and combine with the rest of the ingredients. Serve in pita bread with alfalfa sprouts.

Serves 4.

OLIVE AND ONION SPREAD

8   oz. cream cheese

$^2/_3$ cup sliced black olives

$^1/_2$ small red onion, chopped

Soften the cream cheese and mix with the olives and onions. Serve on pumpernickel bread with sliced tomatoes and shredded lettuce or sprouts.

Serves 4.

NUTTY CREAM CHEESE

8   oz. cream cheese

$^1/_2$ cup green olives, sliced

$^1/_2$ cup walnuts, broken in small pieces

2   T. olive juice

Soften the cream cheese and combine with olives, walnuts, and olive juice. Serve on rye or pumpernickel bread with alfalfa sprouts.

Serves 4.

BACK PACK DINNERS

(continued on next page)

(Backpack Dinners continued)

Mountains should be climbed with as little effort as possible and without desire. The reality of your own nature should determine the speed. If you become restless, speed up. If you become winded, slow down. You climb the mountain in an equilibrium between restlessness and exhaustion. Then, when you're no longer thinking ahead, each footstep isn't just a means to an end but a unique event in itself. This leaf has jagged edges. This rock looks loose. From this place the snow is less visible, even though closer. These are the things you should notice anyway. To live only for some future goal is shallow. It's the sides of the mountain which sustain life, not the top. Here's where things grow. But of course, without the top, you can't have any sides. It's the top that defines the sides.

Zen and the Art of Motorcycle Maintenance by Robert M. Pirsig
Bantam Books, 1974

So why do we do it?
What good is it?
Does it teach you anything?
Like determination? invention? improvisation?
Foresight? Hindsight?
Love?
Art? Music? Religion?
Strength or patience or accuracy or
Quickness or tolerance or
Which wood will burn and how long
Is a day and how far is a mile
And how delicious is water and smoky
Green pea soup?
And how to rely
On your
Self?

On the Loose by Jerry and Renny Russell
Sierra Club Books, 1969

You cannot stay on the summit forever,
You have to come down again...
So why bother in the first place?
Just this:
What is above knows what is below
But what is below does not know what is above.
One climbs, one sees, one descends,
One sees no longer, but one has seen.

There is an art in conducting oneself in the lower regions
By the memory of what one saw higher up.
When one can no longer see
One can at least still know.

by Rene Daumal
(original source unknown, gift from a friend)

THE COMPLETE KITCHEN

Food, glorious food, and what could taste better than pasta pesto with pine nuts, lightly sauteed in extra virgin olive oil, and served at sundown alongside an alpine lake? Careful kitchen organization must precede this meal, and here's how we do it.

We carry two absolutely reliable stoves. We use a Coleman Peak One for the main meal because it can be easily adjusted from simmer to a high boil, it's quick to start and relatively safe, it sits on the ground, and unless we're careless, it's stable. It's quiet, compact, and weighs just over two pounds when it's full. We don't fill it to the limit because white gas expands when it starts to burn, and a full stove will overflow.

Our back-up is a Gaz S200 Bleuet stove that uses butane fuel cartridges. We like it because it's very easy to start, the flame control is good, it burns for approximately two hours, and it rarely malfunctions. The only negatives are the disposable butane containers and the fact that butane produces less heat as the fuel container burns out. The same thing happens in cold weather because less internal pressure means less gas is expelled and thus the flame is cooler. This lightweight stove weighs fifteen ounces and one full cartridge weighs ten ounces.

When we bring the kitchen cupboard to the woods, we limit our pots and pans to one medium-size pot, one small pot with a cover, one Teflon-coated frying pan, one metal mixing bowl, one aluminum pie tin (which does double duty as a cover for the frying pan and the medium-size pot), a small french whip, a small grater, a six-inch-square piece of Plexiglas for a cutting board, one large spoon, one spatula, and finally the requisite pot grip, camp soap, "scrubbie," matches, and kitchen knife. Two kitchen bandanas, or "grunge" bandanas, as we affectionately refer to them, are essentials. We use them for everything from tablecloths and dishtowels to pot covers and handwipes. This looks like a long list, and it is, but the weight is minimum and the efficiency is maximum.

In addition, we consider the First Need Water Pump an important part of our kitchen. If the meal will come to a boil, then we don't purify the cooking water. However, when we add water to mix cheesecakes, pancakes, or puddings, we purify it first.

The "rations bag" adds pizazz to the kitchen. In it, we carry a supply of margarine, olive oil or ghee, brown sugar, dry milk, assorted seeds for garnishes, and labeled film containers filled with vanilla, lemon juice, fancy mustard, cinnamon, nutmeg, garlic, basil, italian herb mix, curry, seasoned salt, table salt, seasoned pepper, and regular pepper. A long list, but once organized, easy to refill and well worth the effort.

We also bring fresh food. These extra treats are not included in the recipes because they're optional and sometimes we serve them and sometimes we don't. The fresh items either will be consumed early in the trip, or they'll be lightweight and hardy. Among them we like to include zucchini, carrots, fresh garlic, a small onion, shallots, and fresh herbs.

Fresh garlic sauteed in virgin olive oil is a small but classy touch, and after one has been on the trail for several days, these little details make the difference between an average and an exceptional dinner. Fresh herbs taste especially good and their near weightlessness makes them a fine addition to the complete kitchen. I did some experiments with herbs, packing them both wet and bone-dry, and found no difference in their long-term freshness. Just a touch of parsley, basil, or garden dill, and a backpacker's dinner is fit for a gourmet.

If the kitchen list seems too long, note that there are

alternative ways of cooking. Once, when I took a six-day solo canoe trip on the Green River in Utah, I chose to avoid the complex complete kitchen. Instead, I ate apples and cold muffins for breakfast, and for dinner, my one-pot meal came from a grocery store soup package . I heated coffee water in a Sierra cup and the total kitchen consisted of two cups and a spoon, one small pot, a stove and matches. It was satisfying, but it didn't taste very good. I learned I'd rather spend extra time preparing a simple dinner and thus enjoy a special meal in a special place.

The last essential in a wilderness kitchen might come as a surprise, but a "headlamp" solves all the problems that arise when dinner is served late and cleanup has to be done in the dark. Even pasta pesto can lose some of its charm when you have to scrape the parmesan from the pot and do the cleanup by touch. With the addition of a headlamp, our kitchen is complete!

CASHEW CALAVO

This recipe is good without the avocado but it's much better with it. An avocado will last until the second night, and since it's heavy, you'll want to eat this meal right away. Remember to pack out the pit.

2	cups instant brown rice
2	cups water
1	package cheese or broccoli soup mix
$1\frac{1}{2}$	cup water
$\frac{1}{2}$	cup instant dry milk
1	avocado
1	cup cashew nuts

At home: in 3 separate bags, pack the brown rice, the soup mix and dry milk, and the cashews. Bag them together in a larger bag along with the optional avocado.

At camp: In a pot with a lid, bring the rice and 2 cups of water to a boil and simmer for 1 minute. Cover tightly and set aside until the rest of the meal is ready. Add $1\frac{1}{2}$ cups water to the soup and dry milk mix and simmer gently, stirring constantly, until the sauce is thick. Serve by layering the chopped avocado, rice, and sauce. Toss the cashews on top.

Serves 4.

Instant Shepherd's Pie

1   5-oz. package dry chipped beef

1   T. dry milk

2   T. dry onion

2   cups Potato Buds

4   T. margarine

1   package instant brown gravy mix

At home: Bag together chipped beef, dry milk, and onions. Put Potato Buds in a separate bag.

At camp: Boil 2 cups of water, add the beef, dry milk, and onions and simmer 2 minutes. Turn off the stove, add the potatoes, and let it sit, covered, for 10 minutes. Heat the margarine in a frying pan and cook the "hash" on both sides. Boil 1 cup water in the potato pot. Add the instant gravy and cook for 1 minute. Serve the hash with the gravy on top.

Serves 2.

DRIED BEEF AND PASTA

3   packages Lipton Mushroom Cup-a-Soup

½   cup instant dry milk

1   cup elbow macaroni

1   5-oz. package chipped beef, sliced

4   cups water

2   T. margarine

At home: Package Cup-a-Soup, dry milk, and chipped beef together. Put the macaroni in a separate bag.

At camp: Cook the macaroni in 4 cups of water. Do not drain. Add the dry ingredients and simmer for 10 minutes. Stir in the margarine and serve at once.

Serves 3-4.

BEEF AND MACARONI

1   1.9-oz. package mushroom soup mix

1   5-oz. package chipped beef, shredded

1   7 $\frac{1}{2}$-ounce package Kraft Macaroni and Cheese Dinner

$\frac{1}{2}$ cup instant dry milk

3 $\frac{1}{2}$ cups water

At home: Pack the soup mix, chipped beef, dry package from macaroni and cheese dinner, and dry milk in one bag, and the macaroni in another.

At camp: Cook the macaroni in 3 $\frac{1}{2}$ cups water. Do not drain the macaroni! Add the dry ingredients and simmer for 5 minutes. Add more water, if necessary.

Serves 3-4.

COUSCOUS AND BEEF

2   cups couscous

1   5-oz. package chipped beef, sliced

1   small package au jus gravy mix

2   T. margarine

1   small onion

4   cups water

At home: Combine the couscous, chipped beef, and gravy mix.

At camp: Chop onion and saute in margarine. Add 4 cups water and the remaining ingredients. Bring to a boil and simmer for 5 minutes. Let stand for 10 minutes before serving.

Serves 3-4.

PROSCIUTTO PASTA WITH PEAS

1/2   cup freeze-dried peas

1/4   lb. prosciutto ham, sliced

1/2   lb. #3 spaghettini

1   1.4-oz. package of instant alfredo pasta sauce

1/2   cup instant dry milk

3   cups water

1/2   cup parmesan cheese

At home: Package the peas and spaghettini together; put the ham in a second bag; in a third bag, the instant sauce and dry milk; and in a fourth bag, the parmesan cheese.

At camp: Boil 3 cups water. Add the pasta and peas and cook 5-10 minutes until *al dente.* Add the ham, sauce mix, and dry milk, and stir over low heat until thick. Serve with parmesan cheese.

Serves 3.

Mung Bean Stew

An oldie for Tripping Lightly that dates back to our "green and brown" days. The stew tastes better than its name might indicate. Corn pancakes (see Breads) are a great complement.

½	cup dry mung beans
¼	cup yellow cornmeal
½	cup dried vegetables
4	T. margarine
4	cups water
1	cup grated cheese

At home: Combine beans, cornmeal, and dried vegetables.

At camp: Bring 4 cups water to a boil. Add the dry ingredients and simmer for 20 minutes or until the beans are tender, stirring occasionally. Remove from stove, stir in margarine, and serve with grated cheese. As with any bean recipe, the cooking time will be shortened by soaking the mung beans prior to cooking them.

Serves 4.

LENTIL CHILI

Don't serve the lentils al dente!

$\frac{1}{2}$	cup lentils
2	T. tomato paste (carry in a film container or other sealed container)
2	T. yellow cornmeal
1	T. chili powder
$\frac{1}{2}$	cup dried mixed vegetables
4	cups water
1	cup grated cheese

At home: Combine all ingredients except cheese.

At camp: Simmer the dry ingredients in 4 cups water for 20-30 minutes, stirring occasionally. Add more water if needed. (The cooking time will be much shorter if you soak the lentils ahead of time.) Serve with grated cheese and corn pancakes or bring along a package of Jiffy Corn Bread Mix and use it to make dumplings for the chili.

Serves 4.

ALPINE RICE

$1\frac{1}{2}$ cups instant brown rice

2 cups water

2 T. margarine

$\frac{1}{2}$ cup parmesan cheese

2 T. instant dry milk

$\frac{1}{2}$ cup grated cheddar cheese

5 oz. chipped beef, sliced

$\frac{1}{2}$ cup dried peas

At home: Combine the rice, beef, and dried peas in one bag. In another bag combine the cheeses and the dry milk.

At camp: Bring the water to a boil. Add the rice, beef, and peas, and simmer for 5 minutes. Set aside, covered, for 10 minutes. Then add the margarine, cheeses, and dry milk, and stir slowly until the cheeses are melted.

Serves 3-4.

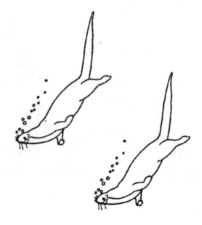

ALPINE GRAINBURGERS

This is as close as we come to a classic burger in the wilderness. We serve it the first night out to enjoy the addition of sprouts, fresh tomatoes, and cucumbers. Be sure to use them on the first night or they'll spoil. A cucumber will keep for a few days if the daytime temperature stays below 80 degrees.

Purchase a grainburger mix in the grocery store, or use a falafel mix. Rehydrate the mix according to the directions on the box, form into patties, and cook slowly in plenty of margarine. Serve in pita bread halves with grated cheese, sprouts, chopped tomato, and cucumber. It tastes especially good when you're surrounded by alpine peaks.

NOODLES AMANDINE

2   4.5 oz. packages of noodles with sour cream mix

1   cup dry milk

4   cups water

$\frac{1}{2}$ cup chopped almonds

4   T. margarine

At home: Combine the noodle mix and the dry milk. Pack the almonds in a separate bag.

At camp: Bring the water to a boil. Add the dry mixture and simmer, stirring occasionally, for 10 minutes. Saute the almonds in margarine. Serve the almonds over the noodles.

Serves 4.

LENTIL-VEGGIE SPAGHETTI

$\frac{1}{2}$	cup lentils
$\frac{1}{2}$	cup dried mixed vegetables
2	T. tomato paste
1	package spaghetti sauce mix
4	cups water
1	lb. #3 spaghettini
$\frac{1}{2}$	cup parmesan cheese

At home: Package the lentils, dry vegetables, and the sauce mix together. Put the tomato paste in a small sealed container (i.e., a film container).

At camp: Combine the dry ingredients with 4 cups water, and simmer until the lentils are soft (approximately 20 minutes). Cook pasta until *al dente,* drain, and combine with sauce. Serve with parmesan cheese.

Serves 4-6.

Falafel over Rice

It takes patience and time to make falafel balls, but the final result is well worth the sticky fingers.

1	6-oz. box falafel mix
½	cup water
2	cups instant brown rice
2	cups water
1	1.9-oz. soup mix (use cheese, broccoli, or mushroom)
½	cup dry milk
2	cups water

At home: In three bags, pack the falafel mix, the brown rice, and the soup and dry milk.

At camp: Combine the falafel and ½ cup water and let sit for 10 minutes. Then form into small balls and saute in margarine. Combine the rice with 2 cups water, bring to a boil, simmer 1 minute and set aside for 15 minutes. Put the rice into individual cups and cook the sauce in the rice pan. To make the sauce, combine the soup and dry milk with 2 cups water and simmer 5 minutes. By now the falafel will be done. Serve the balls over the rice and top with sauce.

Serves 4.

PASTA PESTO

1   lb. #3 spaghettini

1   2.8 oz. tube of pesto

½   cup extra virgin olive oil, or 6 T. margarine (for
      backpacking)

4   cloves fresh garlic, chopped

¼   cup pine nuts

½   cup parmesan cheese

At home: Put the spaghettini in one bag, and the tube of pesto
and garlic cloves in another. Bag the parmesan cheese and
pine nuts separately.

At camp: Cook the spaghettini until *al dente*. Lightly saute the
garlic and pine nuts in the olive oil (or margarine), and add
the pesto sauce. Drain the spaghettini and toss with the pesto
mix and the parmesan cheese. Serve with additional parmesan
cheese.

Serves 4-6.

ALPINE SPAGHETTI

8   oz. rotini pasta

4   T. margarine

$\frac{1}{2}$ cup parmesan cheese

1   t. dry basil (or $\frac{1}{2}$ cup fresh basil)

garlic salt to taste (or 3 cloves fresh garlic)

$\frac{1}{2}$ cup instant dry milk

At home: Package the pasta in one bag and the parmesan cheese, basil, garlic salt and dry milk in another.

At camp: Cook the pasta until *al dente.* Drain off all but one cup of water. Stir in the dry ingredients and margarine and serve with additional parmesan cheese.

Serves 2-3.

SWISS POTATO SOUP

1   1.8-oz. package Knorr Potato Soup with Leeks

1   cup instant dry milk

3   cups water

1   small package freeze-dried peas

$\frac{1}{2}$ lb. swiss cheese, cut into cubes

At home: Combine soup mix, dry milk, and peas. Package the cheese in a separate bag.

At camp: Bring water to a boil and add the soup, dry milk, and peas. Simmer for 10 minutes. Serve with cheese sprinkled on top of the soup. Sunflower seeds make an especially tasty addition. This is also good with Bisquick dumplings.

Serves 4.

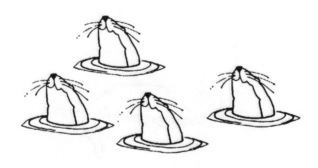

CHICKEN CURRY

$\frac{1}{2}$ cup textured vegetable protein granules, chicken-flavored

2 T. margarine

1 6.9-oz. package Chicken Rice-a-Roni

3 cups water

1 t. to 1 T. curry powder

At home: Combine the vegetable granules, Rice-a-Roni (include the flavor package) and curry powder. Pack condiments separately.

At camp: Bring the water and margarine to a boil and add the vegetable granules, curry powder, and Rice-a-Roni. Cook over low heat for approximately 15 minutes, stirring occasionally, until the rice is done. (It's important to bring the water to a boil before adding the rice mix.) Serve with some or all of the following condiments: raisins, coconut, peanuts, a small chopped red onion.

Serves 4.

BECKY'S BASIC SOUP

This dish is so easy that it doesn't need a recipe, but it's always been a favorite meal in the back country.

Use any dry soup mix from the grocery store. We prefer Knorr Minestrone Soup Mix. Make the soup according to package instructions and add an appropriate amount of extra water for the addition of pasta, hash-brown potatoes, orzo, or dumplings. This makes a quick, soul-satisfying one-pot meal at the end of a good day. Top with the following:

DUMPLINGS

$\frac{1}{4}$ cup Bisquick per person

water to moisten

Mix and drop small spoonfuls of the mixture into the simmering soup. Cover and cook over low heat for 10-15 minutes.

Serves any number.

Mexican Sauce

1   small onion

2   cloves garlic

1   cup water

1   T. margarine

dash of red pepper

1   film container of tomato paste

1   t. chili powder

salt to taste

Saute onion and garlic in margarine. Add the remaining ingredients and simmer uncovered for 10 minutes. Serve with steamed brown rice and flour tortillas.

Serves 4.

Couscous Pilaf

2	cups couscous
4	cups water
4	cubes chicken bouillon
½	cup dried vegetables
¼	lb. cheddar cheese, cut into cubes
4	T. margarine

At home: Package the couscous, bouillon, and dried vegetables together. Put them in another bag along with the cheese.

At camp: Bring the water to a boil, add couscous, bouillon, dry vegetables and margarine, and simmer for 10 minutes. Let stand covered for 5 minutes, then remove from stove and stir in the cheese. Serve when the cheese melts.

Serves 4.

Spanish Rice

1 ½ cups instant brown rice

2   cups water

2   T. tomato paste

1   small onion

1   small green pepper

2   T. margarine

1   t. garlic salt (or fresh garlic)

2   T. chili powder

¼   lb. cheddar cheese, cut into small cubes

salt to taste

At home: Combine rice, garlic, and chili powder in one bag. In a second bag, combine the tomato paste (in a film container), onion, pepper, and cheese.

At camp: Saute the onion, garlic, and pepper in margarine. Add water, rice, tomato paste, salt and chili powder, and simmer for 10 minutes. Take off the heat, add cheese, and serve when the cheese melts. Serve this early in the trip and scoop it up with flour tortillas.

Serves 4.

BEEF STROGANOFF

1   1.4 oz. package of stroganoff mix

½   cup dry milk

5   oz. chipped beef, sliced thin

½   cup dried vegetables

1   T. margarine

1½   cups instant brown rice

3   cups water

At home: In three packages combine: the mix, dry vegetables and dry milk; dried beef; and brown rice.

At camp: Saute the sliced dried beef in margarine. Add the mix, dried vegetables, dry milk and 1½ cups water. Simmer, covered, for 10 minutes. Meanwhile, combine the rice and 1½ cups water, simmer for 2 minutes, cover, and set aside for 10 minutes. Serve the stroganoff over the rice.

Serves 4.

Ramen Veggie Saute

1   small onion, chopped

2   cloves garlic, minced

2   T. olive oil or margarine

$\frac{1}{4}$ cup dried veggies

1   package ramen soup

1   cup water

$\frac{1}{3}$ cup toasted almonds

At home: Package the onion and garlic together. In another bag, place the veggies and the soup (break up the noodles). Put the toasted almonds in a third bag.

At camp: Saute the onion and garlic, add the veggies, water, and soup mix and simmer, covered, for 3 minutes. Sprinkle with toasted almonds and serve.

Serves 2.

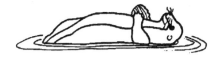

CAMPGROUND DINNERS

(continued on next page)

(Campground Dinners continued)

It is dire poverty indeed when a man is so malnourished and fatigued that he won't stoop to pick up a penny. But if you cultivate a healthy poverty and simplicity, so that finding a penny will literally make your day, then since the world is in fact planted with pennies, you have with your poverty bought a lifetime of days. It is that simple. What you see is what you get.

Pilgrim at Tinker Creek by Annie Dillard
Harper's Magazine Press, 1974

THE CONVENIENT CAR

I never met a bear that could open the trunk of my
Dodge Colt. I like to put food away at night knowing it
will still be there for breakfast. A food bag hanging in a
tree will never be one hundred percent safe from predators, but unless someone steals my Colt in the dark, I
know the food is safe in the trunk.

There's no wisdom in leaving food inside a car in full
view of nocturnal prowlers, because camp rangers are
full of horror stories about large mammals and how they
smash car windows when they spot unguarded food.
The closest I ever came to losing access to my food was
the time I flushed the van keys down the toilet. Because
my adrenalin threw my reflexes into split-second action,
and my fingernails clung to the ridge of my house key
just as the whole ring was about to be sucked into obscu-
rity, we still had dinner on time that night.

Keeping track of the keys is one of the most challeng-
ing parts of my job as guide/chef/chauffeur. I've never
locked them in the trunk, but I used to hide them in a
safe place at night, and completely forget where I put
them next morning. Fortunately, for the sake of my
sanity and professional reputation, after twenty years I
developed a system. I know it works, because I haven't
"lost" the keys for nine years.

It's convenient to have wheels close-by, and compared to backpacking and other forms of remote wilderness camping, established campgrounds offer three
important advantages. We bring frozen dinners prepared
at home, so meals like beef burgundy, first night chili,
and chicken tarragon stew become part of the cook's
repertoire. *The Upscale Outdoor Cookbook* has many short-
order recipes to prepare tableside, but after a strenuous
hike, even the guide prefers resting, reading, or sitting to
cooking.

A large frozen meal in a pot will keep from two to three days in a cooler, and we can extend that time by sealing the cooler with plumber's grey tape until it's time for the meal. In normal summer weather, I've kept a frozen dinner in a cooler for four days. This works best when the cooler is in the trunk of the car, the car is out of direct sunshine, and the daytime temperature stays below eighty.

On the other hand, we often heat brownies and other desserts brought from home on the warm engine under the hood of the car when we return to camp. Then at dessert time, we bring out ice cream from a second cooler, and serve warm pie a la mode. That's the secret to gourmet camp food. Bring an unexpected beef burgundy stew, serve it with something a la mode, and listen to the applause!

The best part of car camping to me will always be the tables. Until I fed twelve backpackers by cooking dinner on two one-burner stoves while sitting on the ground, I didn't appreciate the ease of a picnic table. The backpacker's one-burner stove with a large pot precariously balanced on it, challenges the most seasoned guide, and the exquisite coordination needed to work two stoves at the same time takes some of the fun out of cooking for a group.

I like my traditional two-burner Coleman stove that sits securely on the campground picnic table and when I'm cooking something special, I'm grateful for that substantial base under dinner.

Camper's Fast Beef Stroganoff

1   package (6-oz.) Beef Rice-a-Roni

1   package (5-oz.) chipped beef, sliced

1   small can of mushrooms

3/4   cup sour cream

Cook the Rice-a-Roni according to the package directions. Add the chipped beef, mushrooms, and sour cream. Cover and simmer for 5 minutes.

Serves 3-4.

Chili-Mac Supper

Chili-mac is as close as I'll come in this cookbook to the old-style "canned" camp meals. Served with plenty of grated cheddar cheese and sour cream, this one's pretty good, and easy too!

1   8-oz. package elbow macaroni

1   16-oz. can of chili con carne with beans

1   cup cheddar cheese, grated

tortilla chips

sour cream

Cook macaroni, drain, and mix with chili and cheese. Heat gently until the cheese melts. Serve with tortilla chips, more grated cheese, and sour cream.

Serves 4.

Noodle-Cheese Thing

4   cups water

1   T. vegetable oil

1   lb. elbow macaroni

1/2   pound cheddar cheese, grated

3   11-oz. cans cream of mushroom soup

1   cup peanuts

1   cup sunflower seeds

1   cup pumpkin seeds

1   T. cumin

salt and pepper to taste

Bring the water and oil to a boil. Cook the macaroni until *al dente* and drain off one-half of the water. Stir in the rest of the ingredients and heat slowly.

Serves 8.

DINNER BURRITO

1   large can refried beans

2   T. vegetable oil

1   onion, chopped

1   green pepper, chopped

grated cheddar cheese

sliced avocado

chopped tomatoes

shredded lettuce

sour cream

salsa or picante sauce

flour tortillas

Saute the onion and green pepper in the oil. Add the refried beans and heat slowly. Serve the beans in a warm tortilla with the rest of the ingredients. When you heat the beans, use the oil even if you omit the onions and peppers. Otherwise the beans will stick to the pan.

Serves 4-6.

Garbanzo Bean Curry

2   15-oz. cans garbanzo beans, drained

1   28-oz. can stewed tomatoes

2   chopped onions

4-6 diced potatoes

1   cup raisins

1   T. curry powder

Throw everything in a pot and simmer until the potatoes are tender. Serve with good bread to soak up the juices, or serve it over rice sprinkled with peanuts and coconut.

Serves 6.

WISCONSIN CHEESE FONDUE

*Serve with crusty bread speared with a fork and dipped in the
fondue. You can also dip veggies in the cheese — it's especially good
with broccoli and cauliflower.*

1   lb. cheddar cheese, grated

½   lb. gruyere cheese, grated

2¼ cups flat beer (1½ bottles or cans, average
    12-oz. size)

1½ T. cornstarch

garlic salt to taste

Pour beer into a pan and heat slowly. Gradually stir in the
cheese, mixed with the cornstarch and salt, until the cheese is
melted and the fondue is creamy. (It is very important to stir
continuously and heat slowly to melt the cheese to a smooth
consistency.) Serves 4-6.

MONGOLIAN HOT POT

5   cloves garlic, chopped

1   lb. beef flank steak, sliced thin (you can also use chicken breast or pork)

1   7-oz. jar of hoisin sauce

2   t. cornstarch

1   cup water

3   T. vegetable oil

$\frac{1}{8}$ t. hot crushed red pepper (optional)

6   cups chopped vegetables (broccoli, onion, green pepper and peapods)

1   8-oz. can of water chestnuts, sliced and drained

Saute the meat and garlic in the oil. Mix the cornstarch and water until smooth and add it, along with the hoisin sauce, to the pot and bring to a simmer. Add the vegetables and water chestnuts and simmer, covered, until the vegetables are crisp-tender. Serve over brown rice, bulgar, or couscous.

Serves 4.

ALMOST STROGANOFF

Sometimes recipes are born in unusual circumstances. When my nineteen-year-old son Chris declared that he wouldn't touch anything that "had a mushroom in it," I substituted zucchini, and now we fix "almost" stroganoff.

1	lb. flank steak, cut in strips (freeze steak for an hour before slicing)
2	T. butter or margarine
2	onions, chopped
1	large zucchini, sliced
1	10-oz. can cream of mushroom soup
$\frac{1}{2}$	pint sour cream
salt, pepper	
1	t. basil
$\frac{1}{4}$	t. nutmeg
$\frac{1}{2}$	lb. egg noodles

Saute steak in butter or margarine along with the onions. Toss in the zucchini at the last minute. Stir in soup, sour cream and seasonings, and heat slowly. Cook noodles, drain, and serve the stroganoff over the noodles.

Serves 4.

Arroz Con Pollo

2   chicken breasts, boned and cut in half

3   cloves garlic, chopped

2   onions, chopped

2   T. olive oil

3   stalks celery, sliced

1   T. chili powder

1   16-oz. can stewed tomatoes

1   cup instant brown rice

1   cup water

salt and pepper to taste

Saute chicken, onion, garlic, and celery in olive oil. Add tomatoes and chili powder, and simmer for 20 minutes. Add rice and water, and simmer covered for another 5 minutes (make sure all the rice is immersed in water). Let stand 10 minutes before serving.

Serves 3-4.

Ham and Brie Pasta

1   lb. rotini pasta

1   9-oz. package frozen french-cut green beans

$1/_2$ lb. thinly sliced ham, shredded

$1/_2$ stick butter or margarine

$1/_4$ cup flour

2   cups milk

8   oz. of brie, rind removed and cut into chunks

Cook pasta until *al dente*. Add frozen beans the last five minutes. In another saucepan, melt butter, stir in flour, add milk and stir until the sauce boils and thickens. Remove from heat and stir in brie. Drain pasta and beans. Place in a bowl and toss with the sauce and ham. Serve at once.

Serves 6.

ONE-POT PASTA PRIMAVERA

1   lb. #3 spaghettini

2   cups broccoli florets

1   cup fresh asparagus, cut into 1-inch pieces

2   cups zucchini, sliced

1   10-oz. package frozen peas

½   cup half-and-half, warmed

½   cup parmesan cheese

2   T. butter or margarine

Bring a large pot of salted water to a boil. Add spaghettini and cook for 5 minutes. Add broccoli and asparagus and cook 2 minutes. Add zucchini and peas and cook 3 minutes more. Drain, then toss in a bowl with the half-and-half, cheese, and butter or margarine. Serve with more parmesan.

Serves 6.

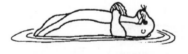

PASTA PRIMAVERA II

1   lb. #3 spaghettini

1   lb. zucchini, sliced

1   lb. ripe tomatoes, chopped

1   onion, chopped

4   garlic cloves, chopped

$\frac{1}{2}$ lb. mushrooms, sliced

$\frac{1}{2}$ cup olive oil

1   T. basil

1   T. italian seasoning

salt to taste

parmesan cheese

Cook the spaghettini until *al dente*. Heat the olive oil in a large frying pan and saute the onion and garlic. Add the zucchini, tomatoes, mushrooms, basil, italian seasoning, and salt, and simmer 10 minutes. Add the sauce to the drained spaghettini and toss. Serve with lots of parmesan cheese.

Serves 4-6.

Ham and Mushroom Pasta

½   lb. mushrooms, sliced

1   lb. boiled ham, sliced

2   onions, sliced

½   stick butter or margarine

4   T. flour

2   10-oz. cans beef consomme

2   t. thyme

1   lb. #3 spaghettini

Saute mushrooms, ham, and onions in the butter or margarine. Add flour and cook briefly over medium heat until the flour bubbles. Add consomme and thyme, and simmer covered, 10 minutes. Cook pasta until *al dente,* drain, mix with the sauce, and serve at once.

Serves 6.

SPAGHETTI CARBONARA

$\frac{1}{2}$ lb. bacon, diced

$\frac{1}{3}$ cup half-and-half

2   eggs

$\frac{1}{2}$ to 1 stick butter or margarine

$\frac{1}{2}$ cup parmesan cheese

1   lb. #3 spaghettini

Fry the bacon until crisp and drain off all but 2 tablespoons of the fat. Add the half-and-half to the bacon pan and keep it warm. Beat the eggs with the parmesan cheese. Cook the pasta until *al dente* and drain. In a large bowl, combine the pasta, the cut-up stick of butter or margarine, the bacon sauce, and the egg mixture. Serve at once with additional parmesan cheese.

Serves 4-6.

PASTA WITH MANY CHEESES

$\frac{1}{2}$ cup half-and-half, warmed

4 oz. swiss cheese, grated

4 oz. blue cheese, crumbled

4 oz. cheddar cheese, grated

$\frac{1}{2}$ cup parmesan cheese

$\frac{1}{2}$ to 1 stick butter or margarine

1 lb. #3 spaghettini

Cook spaghettini until *al dente*. Drain and toss immediately with the warm half-and-half, cheeses, and butter or margarine. Serve at once.

Serves 4-6.

Pasta Puttanesca

1   lb. #3 spaghettini

$\frac{1}{2}$ cup olive oil

4   cloves garlic, minced

2   cups tomato sauce

$\frac{1}{2}$ t. Tabasco sauce

2   T. pesto base

$\frac{1}{2}$ T. oregano

$\frac{1}{4}$ cup sliced black olives

2   oz. black caviar

Cook the pasta until *al dente* and drain. Saute garlic briefly in olive oil. Add tomato sauce, Tabasco, pesto base, oregano, and olives. Bring to a simmer. Gently stir in the caviar and add the pasta to the sauce. Serve at once.

Serves 4-6.

10-MINUTE PASTA ALFREDO

¼   lb. prosciutto, sliced

1   14-oz. can artichokes, drained and cut into small
    pieces

1   1.4-oz. package instant alfredo sauce

2   cups milk

½   lb. #3 spaghettini

parmesan cheese

Slowly heat the milk and stir in the alfredo sauce mix. When it
boils, simmer for five minutes. Meanwhile, cook the pasta
until *al dente*. Drain and toss with artichokes, prosciutto, and
sauce. Serve at once with parmesan cheese.

Serves 2-3.

Fettucine Cantilena

4   oz. cream cheese

4   oz. blue cheese

2   T. butter or margarine

1   large onion, diced

1   cup chicken broth

1   cup shredded prosciutto

½   cup chives (dried or fresh)

freshly ground pepper

1   lb. fettucine

Saute onion in the butter or margarine. Add chicken broth, simmer briefly, add cheeses, and stir until blended. Then add prosciutto, chives, and pepper. Cook the fettucine in boiling water until *al dente*. Drain and add to the sauce. Toss everything together and serve at once.

Serves 4-6.

PASTA AL CAVOLFIORE

4   T. olive oil

1   small cauliflower, cut into bite-size pieces

6   cloves garlic, chopped

1   T. italian seasoning

3   cups tomato sauce

salt and pepper to taste

2   T. butter or margarine

2   cups parmesan cheese

1   lb. #3 spaghettini

Briefly saute cauliflower and garlic in the olive oil. Add the seasoning and the tomato sauce, and simmer 15 minutes. Cook spaghettini until *al dente*. Drain and toss with the butter and one cup of the cheese. Serve the pasta in individual bowls, and spoon the sauce over it. Serve with the remaining cheese.

Serves 4-6.

PASTA WITH TOMATO SAUCE AND WALNUTS

1 cup walnuts

3 T. olive oil

2 cloves garlic, minced

2 shallots, minced

2 T. tomato paste

1½ cups water

2 T. pesto base

salt and pepper to taste

1 lb. #3 spaghettini

½ cup parmesan cheese

Saute walnuts, garlic, and shallots in the olive oil. Add tomato paste, water, and pesto base. Simmer 5 minutes and remove from heat. Cook the spaghettini until *al dente*. Drain. Add the warm sauce and heat together briefly. Add the parmesan cheese, stir, and serve with more cheese.

Serves 4-6.

Linguine with Beer-Cheese Sauce

$\frac{1}{2}$ lb. linguine

1 onion, chopped

2 cloves garlic, diced

3 T. butter or margarine

3 T. all-purpose flour

1 t. worcestershire sauce

$1\frac{1}{2}$ cups milk

8 oz. cheddar cheese, grated

$\frac{1}{2}$ cup beer

salt and pepper to taste

Cook linguine in boiling water until *al dente*. Drain. Saute onion and garlic in butter or margarine, and stir in flour. Add milk all at once and cook until it is thick and bubbling. Add worcestershire sauce and beer and gradually blend in the cheddar cheese. Toss with the linguine and serve at once.

Serves 4.

Pasta with Garlic, Olives, and Artichokes

This was the first campground pasta dinner we invented. Artichokes, olive oil, and garlic sounded like a tasty combination, and since we had some black olives left from lunch, we tossed them in too. Here's the result.

6	cloves garlic, chopped
½	cup olive oil
½	6-oz. can pitted black olives, sliced
2	14-oz. cans artichokes, sliced
1	cup parmesan cheese
1	lb. # 3 spaghettini

Saute the garlic in the olive oil. Keep warm. Cook the spaghettini according to package instructions until *al dente*. Drain. In a large bowl, toss the pasta with the warm olive oil/garlic mix, olives, artichokes, and parmesan cheese. Serve at once with more cheese.

Serves 4-6.

PASTA WITH BROCCOLI

1½ lbs. broccoli

3   cloves garlic, thinly sliced

½   cup virgin olive oil

salt and freshly ground pepper to taste

1   lb. #3 spaghettini

1   cup parmesan cheese

Cut broccoli, including trimmed stalks, into bite-size pieces. Cook broccoli and spaghettini together in boiling salted water for 10 minutes. Heat olive oil, garlic, salt and pepper. Drain the broccoli/pasta mix, toss with the heated oil and ½ cup parmesan cheese. Serve at once with the remaining cheese.

Serves 4-6.

DINNERS FROM HOME

Why

Aware of untold risk
More cognizant of wonder
The mountaineer climbs on above
The humdrum life of everyday
And pits his skill against the alpine way.

Some, far below ask why
Expose a life in worthless cause?
But life without a challenge is just
An empty dance.
What better way for living than by
Choice and not by chance?

J. H. Lindsey, from "Summit," May 1969
taken from *Summits of the Soul* by Patricia K. Armstrong
Naperville Sun, 1978

One of the best paying professions is getting ahold of pieces of country in your mind, learning their smell and their moods, sorting out the pieces of a view, deciding what grows there and why, how many steps that hill will take, where this creek winds and where it meets the other one below, what elevation timberline is now, whether you can walk this reef at low tide or have to climb around, which contour lines on a map mean better cliffs or mountains. This is the best kind of ownership and the most permanent.

It feels good to say, "I know the Sierra," or "I know Point Reyes." But of course you don't—what you know better is yourself, and Point Reyes and the Sierra have helped.

On the Loose by Jerry and Renny Russell
Sierra Club Books, 1969

The Demise of Green and Brown Food

The beginning of the end of Tripping Lightly's green and brown food era was the night I cooked fake beef stew at the Rock Harbor Campground on Isle Royale National Park. We'd been backpacking on the Island for seven days, and this was our final banquet. No one ate it.

I could say that the stew was wonderful and the group was full of grocery store potato chips and Oreos, and that's half true, but the real reason they let it sit in their Sierra cups was because it was awful. One of my vegetarian friends had recommended a certain soy product that allegedly tasted like steak. Better yet, the stuff was fibrous so that when you chewed it, it supposedly turned into something very like a medium-rare porterhouse.

Steak it wasn't, and I've long since forgotten the recipe, but I clearly recall starting the stew in our dinner pot and watching it grow. Too bad it was inedible because it could have fed everyone in the Rock Harbor Campground. We kept adding liquid to those brown dog-food nuggets and they kept right on expanding until we had filled every cooking pot in camp. We ate at the restaurant that night.

When I started Tripping Lightly, I was an ovo-lacto-vegetarian for all the politically correct reasons, plus a few of my own. I brought those personal beliefs into the business and advertised "vegetarian meals" in the early fliers. I knew meat-eaters would eat vegetarian food, and since vegetarians won't eat meat, I figured I could please most of the people, most of the time. In the past eleven years the business has changed and so have I. The recipes in *The Upscale Outdoor Cookbook* reflect a slide from a purist perspective (and mung bean stew) to today's collection of both vegetarian and non-vegetarian recipes. When I was testing some of the dinners, I took the "cassoulet" to an old friend's house. She took one look at me and the chunks of smoked sausage in the pot and laughed. She said, "I never thought I'd see Cari Taylor-Carlson eat sausage again!"

This eclectic recipe collection mirrors my eclectic lifestyle. Green and brown meals limit my kitchen creativity, and I'm too old and mellow to walk the narrow path of the politically correct.

QUICK MINESTRONE

This recipe comes from a cookbook published by the California Wine Council in the 1950s. Serve with lots of good bread.

1   27-oz. can red kidney beans

garlic, salt and pepper to taste

4   cups chopped vegetables (zucchini, celery, onions, carrots, et al)

1   8-oz. can tomato sauce

2 $\frac{1}{2}$ cups water

$\frac{1}{2}$ cup sherry

Mix everything together and simmer, covered, for 1 hour. Makes a quick, thick soup. Add cooked pasta for more calories, if you wish.

Serves 3-4.

Beef Burgundy Stew

Serve with crusty french bread.

3   lbs. stew meat, cut in bite-size pieces

6   cloves garlic

$\frac{1}{2}$ stick butter or margarine

2   10 $\frac{1}{2}$-oz. cans beef consomme

2   cups red wine

2   T. dry basil

salt and pepper to taste

2   T. cornstarch

$\frac{1}{4}$ cup warm water

6   carrots, sliced in chunks

4   potatoes, cubed

3   stalks celery, diced

2   large onions, sliced

Saute beef and garlic in butter or margarine. Add consomme, wine, basil, salt and pepper. Simmer for 1$\frac{1}{2}$ hours. Add carrots, potatoes, celery, and onions, and simmer for another hour. Mix cornstarch and water together, stir into stew, and simmer until thickened.

Serves 8-10.

Mona's Beef Stew Deluxe

3   lbs. beef stew meat (fat removed)

1   11 1/2-oz. can onion soup

1   11 1/2-oz. can cream of mushroom soup

1   8-oz. can sliced mushrooms

1   cup Mogen David wine (not just any old red!)

1   lb. carrots, cut into 1/2- inch pieces

4   onions, sliced

Put everything in a tightly covered roaster and cook at 325° for 3 hours. Stir occasionally. Serve with noodles.

Serves 6-8.

CHICKEN TARRAGON STEW

Be careful not to overcook the pasta. It will continue to cook after the pot has been removed from the stove.

¼	cup butter or margarine
1	onion, sliced
3	cloves garlic, chopped
2	lbs. chicken breast, cut for stir-fry (skin removed)
6	carrots, sliced
1	t. dry tarragon

salt and pepper to taste

2	cups water
2	cups chicken broth
2	t. lemon juice
½	lb. rotini pasta

Saute chicken, onion, and garlic in butter or margarine. Add carrots, tarragon, salt and pepper, water, chicken broth and lemon juice, and bring to a boil. Stir in the pasta and cook, uncovered, for 12 minutes.

Serves 6.

Coq au Vin

Serve with lots of good bread.

2	boned chicken breasts, cut in half
$\frac{1}{2}$	stick butter or margarine
4	cloves garlic
$\frac{1}{3}$	cup brandy
1	cup white wine
1	cup chicken broth
	salt and pepper to taste
2	t. marjoram
6	carrots, cut in chunks
2	onions, cut in chunks
3	potatoes, cut in chunks

Saute chicken and garlic in butter or margarine. Pour brandy over the chicken and ignite. When the flame subsides, add wine, broth, seasonings, carrots, onions, and potatoes, and simmer for 45 minutes.

Serves 4.

Hungarian Goulash (Chicken)

6   chicken breasts, cut in half with skin removed

$\frac{1}{2}$ lb. bacon, sliced

3   onions, sliced

$\frac{1}{2}$ t. dill

$\frac{1}{2}$ t. caraway

salt and pepper to taste

1   29-oz. can sauerkraut

2   T. brown sugar

1   16-oz. can stewed tomatoes

1   cup white wine

sour cream

Fry bacon, set aside, and saute the onions and chicken in the bacon fat. Remove the chicken and pour off all but 3 tablespoons of the fat. Add the seasonings, sauerkraut, sugar, tomatoes, and white wine. Stir, add chicken, and simmer for one hour. Serve with sour cream.

Serves 6.

Hungarian Goulash (Beef)

1/4 cup vegetable oil

5 large onions, cut in rings

3 lbs. good-quality beef stew meat

salt to taste

1 T. sweet paprika

1/2 t. caraway seeds

2 T. tomato paste

1/2 t. crushed hot red pepper (or to taste)

2 10-1/2 oz. cans beef consomme

1 pint sour cream

Saute onions and beef in the oil. Add the rest of the ingredients, cover, and simmer for 3 hours, or until the meat is tender. Cook uncovered the last hour to thicken the sauce. Stir in sour cream and serve over noodles.

Serves 8.

First-Night Chili

1   28-oz. can stewed tomatoes

1   15-oz. can red kidney beans (do not drain)

1   15-oz. can whole kernel corn (do not drain)

2   T. chili powder (or more, to taste)

salt and pepper to taste

1   cup red wine

8   cups chopped vegetables (carrots, celery, broccoli, onion, green pepper, bok choy, zucchini, cauliflower, etc.)

Throw everything into a large pot and simmer until the vegetables are crisp-tender. Serve with grated cheese and sour cream.

Serves 6-8.

BASQUE CHICKEN

6   ripe tomatoes, cut into eighths

3   T. vegetable oil

3   chicken breasts, cut in half

2   onions, chopped

2   green bell peppers, cut in strips

3   cloves garlic, chopped

salt and pepper to taste

Heat oil in a frying pan and brown the chicken. Then saute the onion and garlic in the pan with the chicken. Add green pepper and tomatoes, and season with salt and pepper. Simmer covered for 20 minutes. Serve the chicken over brown rice.

Serves 4-6.

BEEF STIFFADO

2 T. vegetable oil

2 lbs. good quality beef stew meat

2 cloves garlic, sliced

2 large onions, chopped

2 sticks cinnamon

½ cup beef broth

1 cup tomato sauce

½ cup dark beer

salt and pepper to taste

Saute the garlic, beef, and onions in the oil. Add the rest of the ingredients and simmer, covered, for 3 hours or until the meat is tender. Remove cinnamon sticks and serve with noodles or boiled potatoes.

Serves 4.

Almost Cassoulet

2   T. oil

2   onions, chopped

2   carrots, sliced

2   cloves garlic, minced

6   whole chicken breasts, skin removed, cut into quarters

$\frac{1}{4}$ cup tomato paste

$1\frac{1}{2}$ cups white wine

2   16-oz. cans white beans (or precooked white beans)

2   t. oregano

6   smoked sausage links, sliced into chunks

salt and pepper to taste

Heat oil. Add garlic, onions, and carrots and saute briefly. Add chicken and saute until brown on all sides. Remove chicken from the cooking pot and add tomato paste, wine, beans, seasonings, and sausage. Mix well, bring to a simmer, return chicken to the pot, and simmer 30 minutes. Correct seasonings and serve with crusty french bread.

Serves 6

BREADS

Did you ever see a sunrise turn the sky completely red?
Do you sleep beneath the moon and stars, a pine bough
   for your head?
Do you sit and talk with friends, though a word is never
   said?
Then you're just like me and you've been on the loose?

There's a trail that I'll be hiking just to see where it might
   go
Many places yet to visit, many people yet to know,
For in following my dreams I will live and I will grow,
And tomorrow I'll be out there on the loose.

So in search of love and laughter I'll be traveling cross
   this land
Never sure of where I'm going, for I haven't any plan
And in time, when you're ready, come and join me, take
   my hand,
And together we'll find life out on the loose.

   Chorus:
   On the loose to climb a mountain
   On the loose where I am free
   On the loose to live my life
   The way I think my life should be
   For I only have a moment
   And a whole world yet to see
   I'll be looking for tomorrow
   On the loose!

Song from Girl Scout National Center West,
Ten Sleep, Wyoming, 1979.

The Joy of Camping

Epicurus was a hedonist. He wrote, "We call pleasure the alpha and omega of a blessed life. Pleasure is our first and kindred good." I've been in the adventure travel business for eleven years because I feel intense delight when I pack my gear and head for the wilderness. I want to share this good feeling.

Melville said it so well in *Moby Dick* : "Whenever I find myself growing grim about the mouth; whenever it is a damp, drizzly November in my soul; whenever I find myself involuntarily pausing before coffin warehouses, and bringing up the rear of every funeral I meet; and especially whenever my hypos get such an upper hand of me that it requires a strong moral principle to prevent me from deliberately stepping into the street, and methodically knocking people's hats off—then I account it high time to get to sea as soon as I can."

It's good to sit quietly somewhere in a wild area and let the surrounding stillness of the place connect with the stillness in each of us. This intense concentration on the moment never fails to calm my nerves and to bring me pleasure. Compared to Melville's sea, camping gives us a chance to see our surroundings with newborn perspective. Picture a walk down a woodland trail in early morning. You come upon a single ray of sunlight trapped inside a dewdrop on a leaf. Your senses respond. The forest encircles you. Sight, sounds, smells, the softness of the path, all focus like a prism and for a moment, you and the light and the dewdrop and the leaf merge. Then you remember it's Saturday, time to make gingerbread pancakes for breakfast, and the moment disappears but the feeling remains. Ah, life, finding an unexpected moment and savoring the joy! Here are some of my most vivid memories:

• The first time I took a group backpacking in Three Sisters Wilderness in Oregon, and as we watched the sun set, multiple peaks, all the way back to Mount Hood, were illuminated by the rosy alpenglow;

• A solo canoe venture into the Boundary Waters in Minnesota when I looked back across the lake and saw our nine canoes in a row;

• Arriving at Bryce Canyon in Utah in a driving rainstorm and temperatures in the low 40s; we said, "We came to hike, let's hike!" and the rain stopped and the temp rose and the pink hoodoos were magic in the mists that followed the storm;

• When the tide came in around twelve of us sitting on one massive log on the beach at La Push in Olympic National Park and we became aware of how vulnerable we were next to that powerful force;

• Hiking in Pictured Rocks National Lakeshore in Michigan, again at the tail of a storm, when spring pink ladyslippers, brilliant mosses, and a solo wood thrush songster left us speechless, walking in reverent silence;

• An awe-inspiring sunrise at the North Rim of the Grand Canyon, where a small boy who was holding his dad's hand looked across the canyon at the light and asked, "What are we looking at?";

• The day we climbed the wrong mountain outside Jackson, Wyoming, and instead of ascending Jackson Peak, found ourselves next to it, with the entire Jackson Valley spread out six thousand feet below.

Today we watch mountain climbers and river runners on videos and thanks to television, natural history literacy continues to improve. National Geographic's programs have a positive impact on public understanding of ecological systems. Some people actually prefer nature on TV. It's hygenic, it doesn't rain, and armchair adventures are safe.

If we do spend time in a wild area, the experience will

slow us down. It will open our senses and sharpen awareness so we can understand the natural world with our hearts as well as our heads.

Look at what you can see when you "see." Discover the infinitesimally tiny details found in a vernal pond. Take a $1.50 hand lens, a sieve, and a cup to a wetland in May and begin to unravel the complex adaptations of tiny critters and the infinite strands of interdependence. Lost in the intricacies of a cup of pond water, the frustrations and trivial pursuits of city life fade and disappear. Joy and contentment replace freeway traffic jams, crowded schedules, and stress.

What would Epicurus say? I can speak only for myself. The simple act of pitching a tent and the subsequent quiet contemplation fill me with joy and pleasure. This is good!

Insta-breads: Cornbread, Biscuits, and Muffins

You might turn up your nose at instant cornbread at home, but on the trail, served with lentil chili, or a hearty soup, this makes a fine meal. We also use these commercial mixes to make quick dumplings for our soup suppers.

At home: Bag the instant mix with dry milk and dry egg replacers, following each individual recipe.

At camp: Mix in enough water to make a stiff dough. Shape into small patties, or fill a pan with one large patty. Cook in a well-oiled, covered pan over low heat (be sure to oil the lid too). Only turn once. This method will work for commercial mixes such as Bisquick and any of the Jiffy mixes.

Fry Bread

4   cups flour

1   t. salt

1   T. baking powder

water

oil

At home: Combine flour, salt and baking powder.

At camp: Add water to the dry mix to make a stiff dough and knead it until it is smooth and elastic. Form into thin small patties and fry in oil.

Serves 8-10.

DOUGHBOYS

This is the shortest recipe in this book and possibly the best!

Wrap store-bought biscuits around the end of a greased green stick. Cook slowly over coals. Dip into melted butter and then into cinnamon sugar.

ASH CAKES

Use a commercial cornbread mix and prepare the dough according to package instructions. The dough needs to be stiff, so add slightly less water than the recipe calls for. Form into small round patties, about ½ an inch thick, and cook directly on the hot coals. Turn once. Remember to brush off the ashes before eating!

BANNOCK

Make this into a backpacker's recipe by replacing the milk with dry milk powder and adding water on the trail.

1   cup Bisquick mix

½   cup raisins

½   to 1 cup grated cheese

milk

Combine the dry ingredients and moisten with milk to make a stiff dough. Place in a well-oiled frying pan, cover, and cook over low heat, turning once, until the biscuit is cooked through.

Serves 4.

Cinnamon Crisps

flour tortillas

oil

cinnamon sugar

Cut tortillas into quarters and fry them in hot oil until golden brown. Place cinnamon sugar in a brown paper bag. Drop the hot tortillas into the bag and shake to coat them with sugar.

Decadent Donuts

Don't forget to cook the holes!

24　store-bought biscuits

1　quart vegetable oil

cinnamon sugar in a brown bag

Cut a hole in each biscuit with the top of the oil bottle. Heat oil and drop a biscuit into the hot oil until brown on both sides, turning just once. Drop the hot donut into the brown paper bag of cinnamon sugar and eat at once.

CORN PANCAKES

They're filling. We often serve them with lentil chili.

1	cup yellow cornmeal
½	cup whole-wheat flour
½	cup wheat germ (optional)
½	cup dry milk
½	cup raisins
¼	cup brown sugar
1½	cups water (approximate)

salt to taste

At home: Combine all of the dry ingredients.

At camp: Slowly add the water to the dry mix until it is the consistency of thick pancake batter. Cover and cook slowly in plenty of oil, butter, or margarine until done. Serve with more brown sugar.

Serves 4.

Hush Puppies

2   cups cornmeal

2   T. flour

1   cup milk

2   eggs

2   t. baking powder

1   small onion, minced

cooking oil

salt to taste

Combine dry ingredients. Beat eggs and add milk and eggs to the dry mix. Add the minced onion. The mixture should be stiff enough to shape into balls. Drop into hot oil and cook until golden brown.

Serves 4-6.

WHOLE-WHEAT CAMPFIRE BREAD

1   cup warm water

1   package dry yeast

2   T. honey or brown sugar

2   to 3 cups flour ($\frac{1}{2}$ whole-wheat and $\frac{1}{2}$ unbleached white is best)

Combine yeast, warm water, and sugar or honey and stir until yeast is dissolved. Then mix all ingredients together and knead well. Let dough rise in a well-oiled frying pan, topped with another pan for a lid. Oil both the frying pan and the "lid." (The point of this arrangement is to be able to flip the pan over so that the bread cooks on both sides on the coals.) When the bread has risen, place the pan directly on the hot coals and cook for 8 minutes. Do not place on flames; the bread will burn. Turn carefully and cook the other side for another 8 minutes. Remove from the fire and let bread cool for a few minutes before giving it a good thump to loosen both sides from the pan.

Serves 4-6.

BACKPACK DESSERTS

I realized that the true value of a trail has little to do with efficiency of movement. It has more to do with how alive one becomes there, how fully awake and sensibly rooted in the place. When I look back over the trails I have walked, through forests and over mountains, down streams and rivers, along the edge of the sea, I am grateful for their kindness, always severe and gentle at the same time. Like the best of teachers, they have prodded me to know myself, to ask why I am here for this brief moment on earth.

When you think about it, you walk mostly in the same places and along the same paths every day. Look at the way the rugs are worn, or the areas where your constant tracking has kept the floor clean in your house. People like to follow patterns, crossing the grass at the same spot, always walking between these two trees and not the next two over in the row. We are creatures of habit for the most part. This is what trails are all about. We like consistency and predictability, so we make a trail.

Thomas James *The Colorado Express*, Volume XIII
Denver, Colorado, 1978

Where the Sidewalk Ends

There is a place where the sidewalk ends
And before the street begins,
And there the grass grows soft and white,
And there the sun burns crimson bright,
And there the moon-bird rests from his flight
To cool in the peppermint wind.

Let us leave this place where the smoke blows black
And the dark street winds and bends.
Past the pits where the asphalt flowers grow
We shall walk with a walk that is measured and slow,
And watch where the chalk-white arrows go
To the place where the sidewalk ends.

Yes, we'll walk with a walk that is measured and slow
And we'll go where the chalk-white arrows go,
For the children, they mark, and the children know,
The place where the sidewalk ends.

Where the Sidewalk Ends by Shel Silverstein
Harper & Row, 1974

Snowbank Creme and Other Desserts

"Life's uncertain, eat dessert first." A friend and fellow adventurer regularly enjoys a chocolate Dove Bar before dinner and a glass of wine. He and his wife are world travelers who enjoy canoeing, backpacking, hiking, biking, cross-country skiing, and life! A pre-dinner Dove Bar becomes an appropriate symbol for a life filled with joyful adventure travel.

This couple would have appreciated the creme caramel we made in a snowbank in Oregon in the Three Sisters Wilderness Area. When I have to pack one hundred pounds of food into meal-size portions, label each baggie, and put cooking instructions inside every package, I'm apt to get a little crazy. In the rush of packing food for twelve backpackers for eight days, I bought a Knorr Creme Caramel Dessert Mix without carefully reading the outside of the package first. I overlooked the instructions which said to put the caramel sauce "in the freezer" for ten minutes so it would coat the pot. Could we improvise refrigeration when we had no facilities, and the daytime temperature seldom dipped below seventy degrees? I decided to overlook the details and worry about freezers later.

When we backpack, we count days and desserts, and eventually the time came to serve the caramel treat. That year an unusually heavy snowfall combined with a late melt had left snowbanks for us to cross as we hiked in the mountains. We found plenty of packed snow trailside, but not much at our campsites. A decent snowbank, I knew, was just what we needed for the creme caramel.

On the sixth night we camped next to Squaw Creek and set up our kitchen on a bank above the cascading river with the Middle Sister in the foreground and the North Sister in the background. Right in our kitchen was a snowbank so it was time to make creme caramel. First, we coated the frying pan, our dessert bowl, with caramel sauce; then we dug a matching hole in the snow and placed the pan in the "freezer" for the required ten minutes. I made the custard and we poured it into the now-frozen caramel mold, set the pan back into the makeshift freezer, covered it with more snow, and left it alone. At dessert time we unmolded it with fear and trembling. It was perfect. Our creme caramel looked just like the photo on the box—only better, because our dining room was wallpapered with mountains and the background music was provided by water crashing over ledges.

We camped at Squaw Creek for two nights. When we returned from a hike the following afternoon, the snowbank was gone. Our freezer had melted away in one day without leaving a trace of snow or ice behind to remind us of our serendipitous fortune.

I recall another memorable dessert outside Jackson, Wyoming when we were canoeing on the Oxbow of the Snake River. My friend in Jackson, Kim Fadiman, arranged for canoes and dessert. On the final day of a seven-day Tripping Lightly adventure in Grand Teton National Park, we paddled to a riverbank, tied up the canoes, found a comfortable place to sit, and waited for the sun to set behind Mount Moran. The still river mirrored both the mountain and the sandhill cranes flying overhead. We whispered, afraid to spoil the magic. When it was time for dessert, Kim brought out his cooler, the Kahlua ice cream mix, and a thermos of liquid nitrogen. With an assist from a fearless helper, he poured the nitrogen slowly and carefully into liquid cream, and looking like the quintessential mad scientist, stirred the pot. It steamed, sputtered, frothed, and froze. We were treated to perfectly smooth, crystal-free Kahlua ice cream.

The rest of the story lies with the unique character of

my friend Kim Fadiman, and the dangerous qualities of liquid nitrogen. He buys it at the local sperm bank, where the first time he arrived with his quart-size thermos, the receptionist took one look at him and said, "My, what a donation!"

Liquid nitrogen is not for sale. It's very dangerous and most of it is impure and unsafe for consumption. With a temperature of minus 321 degrees Fahrenheit, it will freeze just about anything within seconds. The difference between dry ice at approximately minus 108 degrees Fahrenheit and liquid nitrogen at minus 321 is dramatic and because we use it in a liquid state, the danger increases exponentially. The damage to human flesh can be instant and severe.

Fortunately, we were in the presence of an expert and an ice cream aficionado who knew that if he chilled the liquid ice cream mixture a minimum of four hours, left it in the freezer for an hour to bring it just to the point when the crystals are ready to form, and then poured in the nitrogen, we would have perfect ice cream, and we did.

He also knew the importance of carefully leaving the cap of his thermos ajar and handling it gently, because a closed cap meant that pressure from escaping gas would blow up his thermos and his car windows, as well! This unique method resulted from the collaboration of three friends who shared a common interest in ice cream. They were aware of the relationship between the length of time it takes to freeze it and the pristine quality of the flawless final product. Kim credits Garniss Curtis, a former geology professor from California, who made the suggestion, "Why not try something really cold, like liquid nitrogen?"

We were the fortunate beneficiaries of this ice cream experimentation which began three years before. My friend is fully cognizant of the risks in his extraordinary technique and his willingness to experiment clearly represents the philosophy, "Life's uncertain, eat dessert first."

The reader is EXPRESSLY WARNED NOT to attempt to use liquid nitrogen in making Riverbank Kahlua Ice Cream or during any other food preparation. Liquid nitrogen is not for resale and is extremely dangerous to humans because it has a temperature of -321° F. Upon even minor contact, liquid nitrogen will freeze virtually everything instantly, and will severely and irreparably damage the human body and/or skin. This author expressly disclaims any potential liability for any damages or injuries caused by anyone attempting to use liquid nitrogen during food preparation.

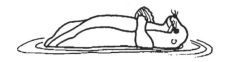

RIVERBANK KAHLUA ICE CREAM

Remember—we DO NOT RECOMMEND using liquid nitrogen!

1   quart half-and-half

1   quart light cream

$^3/_4$ to 1 can of sweetened condensed milk (to taste)

$^1/_4$ t. salt

4   T. instant coffee (add more to taste)

2   ounces Kahlua (to taste)

Stir all ingredients well for a few minutes to dissolve the instant coffee completely . Chill at least 4 hours in the refrigerator and 1 hour in the freezer. Remove from the freezer just before ice crystals begin to form and freeze in a conventional ice cream freezer.

Makes two quarts.

WILDERNESS PIES

Any brand or flavor of instant pudding mix will work in this recipe. For the crust you can use vanilla wafers, oreos, graham crackers, macaroons, etc. The best method is to make the pies in individual cups. Put a $^1/_2$-inch layer of crumb crust in a cup, add the ready-made pudding, and top with more crumb crust. There are many interesting combinations to try.

Rice Pudding

$\frac{1}{2}$ cup instant rice

$\frac{1}{2}$ cup raisins

$2\frac{1}{2}$ cups water

$\frac{1}{2}$ cup dry milk

1   package of "regular" (not instant) vanilla pudding mix

Combine the rice, raisins, and water and simmer for 5 minutes. Add the dry milk and pudding mix; cook and stir until thick.

Serves 4.

Fruit Fritters

1   cup flour

1   t. baking powder

3   T. instant egg replacer

$\frac{1}{3}$ cup dry milk

1   cup dried fruit, chopped

Rehydrate fruit in water. Combine dry ingredients with $\frac{1}{2}$ cup water. Drain fruit and add to the "dry" mixture. Drop by spoonfuls on a hot greased skillet.

Serves 4.

APPLE CRISP

$\frac{1}{4}$	lb. dried apples, cut in small pieces
2	cups water
2	T. butter or margarine
$\frac{1}{2}$	t. cinnamon
1	cup rolled oats (instant)
$\frac{1}{4}$	cup whole-wheat flour
1	T. brown sugar

Rehydrate apples in water. Do not drain. Melt butter in a frying pan and add the undrained apples. Mix the rest of the ingredients and sprinkle over the apples. Cover and cook over low heat for 15-20 minutes.

Serves 4.

DESSERTS OFF THE SHELF

Cheesecake

Caramel Creme

Instant Mousse (add shaved chocolate or chips)

Instant Pudding (add malted milk mix for extra flavor)

Junket

Some of the best camp desserts go straight from the box to the cup. It's easiest to add dry milk and repackage at home, and it's important to stir the instant desserts carefully and briefly, or the mix will turn to soup. Each year the grocer's selection gets better, and it's fun to try out new box mixes. The combinations are endless. Sometimes we add mincemeat to a pudding mix for additional calories and a richer treat.

INDIAN RICE PUDDING

1 ½ cups water

⅓   cup dry milk

1 ½ cups instant brown rice

½   cup raisins

2   T. molasses

2   T. brown sugar

¼   t. cinnamon

⅛   t. ginger

salt

At home: Package the dry milk, rice, and raisins together. Place molasses in a film container.

At camp: Bring the water to a boil, add the rice, raisins, dry milk, and simmer 2 mintues. Set aside, covered for 15 minutes. Add molasses, brown sugar, spices, and eat while it's warm.

Serves 4.

CAMPGROUND DESSERTS

One of the strange things about living in the world is that only now and then is one quite sure one is going to live forever and ever and ever. One knows it sometimes when one gets up at the tender solemn dawn-time and goes out and stands alone and throws one's head far back and looks up and up and watches the pale sky slowly changing and flushing and marvelous unknown things happening until the east almost makes one cry out and one's heart stands still at the strange unchanging majesty of the rising of the sun—which has been happening every morning for thousands and thousands and thousands of years. One knows it then for a moment or so. And one knows it sometimes when one stands by oneself in a wood at sunset and the mysterious deep gold stillness slanting through and under the branches seems to be saying slowly again and again something one cannot quite hear, however much one tries. Then sometimes the immense quiet of the dark blue at night with millions of stars waiting and watching makes one sure; and sometimes a sound of far-off music makes it true; and sometimes a look in someone's eyes.

The Secret Garden by Frances Hodgson Burnett
J. B. Lippincott Company, 1911

ANOTHER BEAR STORY

Back in the late '70s, a well-fed bear lived close to Chimneys Picnic Area in Smoky Mountains National Park. I used to take my four children to the mountains during spring break, and because we slept indoors in cabins outside the Park, we picnicked at Chimneys.

We had great times there and since it's adjacent to the West Prong of Little Pigeon River and Cove Hardwoods Nature Trail, the picnic area is popular and the sites along the river fill early for the evening meal.

One year, at precisely 5:30 p.m. every night, a bear came down the mountainside and made his rounds. He knew the picnickers' habits and timed his arrival to guarantee himself a hot dinner. When we heard "bear!", we investigated, and found one fat, happy Smoky Mountains bear sitting on a picnic table munching the remains of some distraught family's dinner.

After he finished the table food, he kicked their Coleman cooler around until the lid popped open and their food cache spilled out. He ate the margarine, spilled the milk, picked at the leftovers, and left. We could see this was not a stereotypical clumsy bear, but a clever uninvited guest, who moved into a dinner party with confidence, filling his stomach and exiting gracefully before lumbering up the steep side of the mountain. He deserved our respect.

The following night, another group of unsuspecting campers picked up dinner in Gatlinburg. Just as they spread out their Colonel Sanders Kentucky Fried Chicken and readied themselves for the feast, he arrived, right on schedule at 5:30 p.m. Again, we watched this humorous scene, pleased that our spaghetti dinner was safe and feeling smug that the master predator had found them first.

The next night we were ready. Although we knew

our turn was coming, the five of us didn't choose to share our burritos with the bear. Right at 5:30 when he came to our table, we scooped up everything edible, jumped in our orange Volkswagen van, rolled up the windows, readied the cameras, and watched the show. He climbed on the table and did what bears do when they look for food. He didn't stay long because our food was safe in the van.

Inadvertently, we left my daughter Linda's camera on the table and when it was all over and we crept out of the van, Linda picked up her camera, and in an eleven-year-old tone of authentic disgust, said, "Yuk! He slimed on my camera!" We were proud, though. He hadn't got our food and we were able to take photos of him standing on the table just ten feet from the car windows. However, that's not the end of the story.

Ten years later, I went back to the Smokies with a Tripping Lightly group. We sell Tripping Lightly tee-shirts to our customers, and everyone's favorite has printed on it, "Life's Uncertain, Eat Dessert First." The drawing on this tee came from a slide I took that eventful night. It's a picture of that clever bear standing on our table.

When I took my group into the Visitors Center for an orientation, I was wearing the "dessert" tee with the bear picture. It's usual for people to notice the message on a shirt, but as I talked with a park naturalist I noticed him staring at mine. Finally he said, "Gosh, that sure looks just like a Smoky Mountains Chimneys bear." Imagine his surprise when I replied, "It is!"

Today they tranquilize the bears that come to dinner and move them to another part of the Park. That's the best policy, but outwitting him resulted in a great story for my kids to tell back home and I got some unusual art for a Tripping Lightly tee.

LEMON CHEESE MOUSSE

8   oz. cream cheese (softened)

$^3/_4$ cup milk

1   3-oz. package of instant vanilla pudding mix

2   T. lemon peel, finely grated

1   T. lemon juice

Use a wire whip to blend the cream cheese and $^1/_2$ c. of milk until the mixture is very smooth. Add $^1/_4$ cup milk, pudding mix, lemon peel and lemon juice. Stir gently until blended. Do not overbeat!

Serves 4.

AMAZING CHOCOLATE FONDUE

We also like to dip chocolate chip cookies and angel food cake for a double sweet treat!

12   oz. chocolate chips

1   cup whipping cream

1   t. vanilla

     assorted fruits, cut into bite-size pieces

In an improvised double-boiler, heat chips and whipping cream. Add vanilla. Dip fruit into melted chocolate.

Serves 8.

CARAMEL FONDUE

The hardest part of this recipe is unwrapping the caramels.

2   lbs. caramels

1   cup whipping cream

apples cut into wedges

Put caramels and cream in an improvised double boiler and stir until the caramels melt and blend with the cream. Serve by dipping the apples in the melted caramel. You can also dip cookies and cake into the fondue.

Serves 6-8.

BANANA PUDDING

24   vanilla wafers

2   bananas, thinly sliced

1   small package vanilla instant pudding

$1^3/_4$ cups milk

1   4-oz. container of Cool Whip

Using a french whip, make the pudding as directed on the package. Layer cookies and bananas and pour pudding over all. If possible, chill. Let it sit for at least an hour to soften the cookies and to blend the flavors. Spread a layer of Cool Whip over the dessert before serving .

Serves 4.

River-Runner's Shortcake

1   angel food loaf cake or pound cake

fresh fruit

Cool Whip, whipped cream, or vanilla yogurt

Chop fruit and spoon over the cake. Top with Cool Whip, whipped cream, or vanilla yogurt.

Serves 6.

Pan-Fried Apple Dumplings

This recipe was invented one day when the pantry was empty. We also use it to accompany a soup supper by substituting cheese for apples.

1   T. butter or margarine

1½ cups Bisquick mix

2   apples, cored and sliced

sugar

cinnamon

nutmeg

Mix Bisquick with enough water to make a stiff dough. Melt butter or margarine in frying pan and put in dough. Cover with sliced apples and sprinkle with sugar, cinnamon, and nutmeg. Cover and cook over low heat until the dough is cooked through and the apples are beginning to soften.

Serves 4.

Lemon Yogurt Fruit Dip

1   8-oz. carton of lemon yogurt

1   cup sour half-and-half

1   T. brown sugar

1   t. lemon juice

1   t. ginger

freshly grated lemon peel

Combine all ingredients and chill at least an hour to blend the flavors. Serve with fresh fruits.

Serves 6.

Grandma's Rice Pudding

I found this simple recipe, written ninety years ago, in my grandmother's handwritten cookbook, and updated it for the 1990s by using instant rice and substituting Cool Whip for whipped cream.

1   cup instant brown rice

1   cup water

1/4   cup sugar

1   8-oz. can of crushed pineapple, drained well

1   4-oz. container of Cool Whip (or 1 cup heavy cream, whipped with 1 T. sugar)

Combine rice, sugar, and water, and simmer for 5 minutes. Cover the pan and set it aside. After it cools completely, fold in the pineapple and the Cool Whip. Serve at once.

Serves 4.

Desserts from Home

In the first place you can't see anything from a car; you've got to get out of the goddamned contraption and walk, better yet crawl, on hands and knees, over the sandstone and through the thornbush and cactus. When traces of blood begin to mark your trail you'll see something, maybe.

Desert Solitaire by Edward Abbey
Ballantine Books, 1968

One final paragraph of advice: do not burn yourselves out. Be as I am—a reluctant enthusiast . . . a part-time crusader, a half-hearted fanatic. Save the other half of yourselves and your lives for pleasure and adventure. It is not enough to fight for the land; it is even more important to enjoy it. While you can. While it's still here. So get out there and hunt and fish and mess around with your friends, ramble out yonder and explore the forests, encounter the grizz, climb the mountains, bag the peaks, run the rivers, breathe deep of that yet sweet and lucid air, sit quietly for a while and contemplate the precious stillness, that lovely, mysterious and awesome space. Enjoy yourselves, keep your brain in your head, and the head firmly attached to the body, the body active and alive and I promise you this much: I promise you one sweet victory over our enemies, over those desk-bound people with their hearts in a safe deposit box and their eyes hypnotized by desk calculators. I promise you this: you will outlive the bastards.

by Edward Abbey from *The Earth Speaks*, edited by Steve Van Matre
and Bill Weiler
Acclimatization Experiences Institute, 1983

LIFE IN THE SLOW LANE

There's a theory floating around that laughter can be therapeutic. I have found a clear connection between uninhibited playfulness, wilderness camping, and mental health.

A traditional rationale extrapolated by some outdoor schools suggests we learn wilderness camping skills in order to build character and assertiveness, and that only by physical deprivation can we know ourselves. I disagree. Going to the wilderness is meant to be fun. I'm not a clock-watching backpacker who ever remembers how long it takes me to get anywhere. Some people need to do it faster, better, and more efficiently. Why? A wilderness adventure isn't a race, but about letting go.

Once you're there, will it matter if you cleaned the bathroom before you left or whether or not you sent the memo to what's his name about the widgets? They don't install fax machines at northern inland lakes, and there are no telephones equipped with blinking red answering machines to remind us of unfinished business. The world can't follow us into the woods unless we take it with us.

When we hike for several days, we learn about the place where we are—what grows there and why, where the good overlooks and the best places to see eagles are, how to listen to the wind, which path leads to yellow ladyslippers, what's the best lunch stop, and how the breeze feels when it caresses your sweaty face at the top of a hill.

We learn something about ourselves when we discover what we like about a place. I love the austerity of a high desert in Utah, while others need endless space or large bodies of water, and some prefer to hike above the timberline.

When we're out there, it's best to avoid the "if/then" philosophy. If I walk twenty more miles in the rain instead of camping here for the night, then my back-home problems won't seem so important. The if/then process drives people on to greater challenges because "if I scale this obstacle, then I can solve the rest of my life." I wish it worked that way. Some of us are still waiting for the if/then trolley because the ifs are finished and the thens are still to come.

Perhaps Gandhi had the right idea when he wrote, "There is more to life than increasing its speed." Most wilderness travelers with watches Krazy-glued onto their wrists would enjoy a vacation from fifteen-minute beeps. Without a watch, we have no objective scale for time or pace except sunrise and sunset, and it's okay to eat when we're hungry and sleep when we're tired!

Life in the slow lane encourages close communication with the place. The business of getting to the end of the hike shouldn't interfere with the importance of smelling wild roses and picking blueberries along the way. Robert Pirsig wrote in *Zen and the Art of Motorcycle Maintenance*, "To live only for some future goal is shallow. It's the sides of the mountains which sustain life, not the top."

I can't be too serious about wilderness travel. Like the otter who continues to play in adult life, I prefer laughter and giggles to solemn moments. What feels better than a therapeutic belly-laugh, and when do we have more time for silliness but in the woods?

Laughter is an important component of wellness. If adventuresome people have more fun, then aren't we fortunate if we can camp, hike, canoe, ski, and back-pack? It's easy to be serious. Fun requires letting go.

Someone once wrote, "We don't stop playing because we grow old, we grow old because we stop playing." Uninhibited laughter and playfulness won't guarantee a joyful life, and wilderness travel isn't the universal anti-dote for stress, but when I camp, I drink at my fountain of youth.

Lemon Bars

1   package lemon cake mix

3   eggs

1   stick butter or margarine

$\frac{1}{2}$ cup sugar

$\frac{1}{2}$ t. baking powder

$\frac{1}{4}$ t. salt

2   t. grated lemon peel

juice of 2 lemons

Combine 1 egg, butter or margarine, and cake mix. Pat into an ungreased 13-in. x 9-in. x 2-in. pan. Bake at 325° for 20 minutes. Beat 2 remaining eggs, sugar, baking powder, salt, lemon peel and lemon juice until light and foamy. Pour over hot crust. Return to oven and bake at 325° for 25 minutes.

Serves 16.

FRUITCAKE

These cakes require a long list of ingredients, but they keep forever in the refrigerator and are so tasty for dessert on a backpacking or a canoe trip in the wilderness that the results are well worth the extra effort.

2	cups mixed candied fruit
2	cups raisins
1	cup chopped dates
1	cup broken walnuts
1	20-oz. can crushed pineapple, drained
1	cup port wine
$1\frac{1}{2}$	sticks butter or margarine
1	cup brown sugar
$\frac{1}{4}$	t. of nutmeg, cinnamon and clove
4	eggs, well beaten
$2\frac{1}{2}$	cups flour
1	t. baking powder
$1\frac{1}{2}$	t. baking soda
1	t. salt

In a large bowl, combine fruit, raisins, dates, nuts, and pineapple. Pour port wine over the mixture and set aside, stirring occasionally. In a separate bowl, cream butter or margarine, brown sugar and spices, and blend in beaten eggs. Add next four dry ingredients and mix. Stir in fruit and wine. Grease and flour 2 loaf pans, 9-in. x 5-in. x 3-in., and divide batter in them. Bake at 300° for 2 hours, or until a toothpick comes out clean. Wrap in cloths soaked with brandy, then in foil, and store in a cool place. Do not serve for at least 2 weeks.

Apple Pudding

3 cups sliced apples

$\frac{1}{3}$ cup sugar

$\frac{3}{4}$ cup hot water

$1\frac{1}{2}$ cups crushed pineapple, drained

1 cup chopped walnuts

$\frac{1}{2}$ stick butter or margarine

$\frac{1}{2}$ cup brown sugar

1 t. cinnamon

1 cup flour

1 t. baking powder

$\frac{1}{4}$ t. salt

Combine apples, sugar, and water and simmer for 10 minutes. Add pineapple and nuts, and pour into a well-oiled 9-in.-sq. pan. Combine butter or margarine, sugar, cinnamon, flour, baking powder, and salt, and sprinkle over the top of the apple mixture. Bake at 350° for 40 minutes.

Serves 8.

Pineapple Cake

The cake is fabulous served warm with vanilla ice cream.

CAKE:
Combine and mix by hand:

1 $\frac{1}{2}$	cups sugar
2	cups flour
$\frac{1}{4}$	t. salt
2	t. baking soda
2	eggs
1	20-oz. can of crushed pineapple with juice
1	t. vanilla

Pour into an ungreased 9 x 13-in. pan and bake at 350° for 35 minutes.

TOPPING:
Combine in a saucepan:

1	stick butter or margarine
$\frac{3}{4}$	cup sugar
$\frac{1}{2}$	cup evaporated milk
1	cup chopped nuts

Boil for 2 minutes and pour over warm cake.

Serves 16.

Lemon Cake

1   package lemon cake mix

1   3-oz. package lemon Jello

$^3/_4$ cup vegetable oil

$^3/_4$ cup water

4   eggs

CAKE:
Beat all ingredients for 8 minutes. Pour into a well-oiled 9 x 13-in. pan and bake according to the cake mix directions.

TOPPING:
Combine 2 cups of powdered sugar and the juice of 2 lemons. Pour over the cake when you remove it from the oven.

Serves 16.

Almost Candy Bars

1   cup white sugar

1   cup light Karo syrup

2   cups chunky peanut butter

8   cups Special K cereal, corn flakes, or Rice Krispies

12   oz. chocolate chips

12   oz. butterscotch chips

Combine sugar and Karo syrup in a large pot and bring to a rolling boil. Add peanut butter and cereal. Press mixture into a well-oiled 12 x 16- in. pan. Melt chocolate and butterscotch chips together and spread over the cereal mix. Wait until the chocolate hardens before cutting into the bars.

Serves 16.

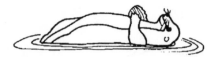

Pecan Special

6   egg whites

1 $\frac{1}{2}$ cups sugar

2   cups chopped pecans

30   Ritz crackers, crushed

1   t. vanilla

6   oz. chocolate chips (12 oz. are better!)

Beat egg whites until frothy. Add sugar slowly and continue beating until all the sugar is added and the egg whites are stiff. Fold in the pecans, crackers, and vanilla and pour into a well-oiled 9-in. sq. pan. Bake at 325° for 50 minutes. Remove from oven and sprinkle the chocolate chips over the top immediately.

Serves 12.

Peanut Butter Squares

1   cup chunky peanut butter

2   cups graham cracker crumbs

3   cups powdered sugar

2   sticks melted butter or margarine

12 oz. chocolate chips

Mix by hand the peanut butter, graham cracker crumbs, powdered sugar and melted butter or margarine, and press into a well-oiled jelly roll pan. Place in refrigerator. Melt the chocolate chips and spread over the cooled pan. Do not cut until the chocolate has set.

Serves 16.

Family Brownies

4   eggs

2   cups sugar

2   sticks butter or margarine

1   t. vanilla

4   squares melted chocolate

1   cup flour

$\frac{1}{4}$ t. salt

$1\frac{1}{2}$ cups broken walnuts

Beat the eggs, sugar, vanilla, and butter or margarine until creamy. Add the melted chocolate. Beat in the flour and salt and stir in the nuts. Bake in a well-oiled 9 x 13-in. pan at 350° for 40 minutes.

Serves 16.

Chocolate-Pecan Pie

2 unbaked commercial "deep dish" pie shells

6 eggs

1 cup sugar

½ cup brown sugar

1½ cups pecans

2 t. vanilla

1½ cups light corn syrup

1½ sticks butter or margarine

12 oz. chocolate chips

2 T. flour

Melt butter or margarine and set aside. Beat eggs and add the rest of the ingredients to the eggs. Add the melted butter. Pour into 2 pie shells and bake at 350° for 60 minutes. Serve warm with a scoop of vanilla ice cream.

Serves 16.

MARY'S BANANA CAKE

Mary Eloranta is a frequent Tripping Lightly guide. Her children, Jesse and Tyler, know it's time for Mom to guide a trip when they find bananas in the freezer!

1	package yellow cake mix
1¼	cups water
⅓	cup vegetable oil
3	eggs
3-4	bananas (unless they're already mushy, freeze the bananas to soften them)
¼	cup granulated sugar

Blend cake mix, water, oil, and eggs. Chop the bananas into small pieces and add them to the batter. Bake in a 9 x 13-in. pan according to instructions on the box. While the cake is still warm, sprinkle with granulated sugar.

MARY'S PECAN PIE BARS

2   cups flour

1   cup brown sugar

2   sticks butter or margarine

5   eggs

1   cup dark corn syrup

$^3/_4$ cup sugar

dash salt

1   t. vanilla

$1^1/_2$ cups broken pecans

Combine flour and brown sugar and cut in two sticks of butter or margarine. Press into an ungreased 9 x 13 in. pan and bake 10-15 minutes at 325°. Combine the rest of the ingredients, pour over the hot crust, and bake 50 minutes at 275°, or until the center is set.

Serves 16.

MARY'S DOUBLE-CHOCOLATE WALNUT BARS

2   sticks butter or margarine

4   squares unsweetened chocolate

2   cups sugar

3   eggs

1   t. vanilla

1   cup flour

1½   cups walnuts

6   oz. chocolate chips

Melt chocolate and butter and beat in sugar with a wooden spoon. Add the eggs, beating after each one. Stir in vanilla, flour, and 1 cup walnuts. Spread into a well-greased 9 x 13-in. pan, sprinkle with the rest of the walnuts and the chocolate chips. Press down lightly and bake 35 minutes at 350° degrees.

Serves 12.

MARY'S CHOCOLATE-IN-BETWEENS

1   cup brown sugar

1 ½ sticks butter or margarine

¼   t. salt

1 ½ cups all-purpose flour

1   cup quick oats

1   14-oz. can sweetened condensed milk

6   oz. chocolate chips

Cream the brown sugar, butter or margarine, and salt. Add flour and oats. Pat half of this mix into a well-greased 9x13-in. pan. In a 2-quart saucepan, combine the condensed milk and chocolate chips and warm over low heat, stirring constantly, until the chips are melted. Pour over the crust in the pan and cover with remaining crumb mix. Bake at 350° for 25-30 minutes.

Serves 12.

CARLSON'S GINGERBREAD

2   sticks butter or margarine, melted and cooled

1   cup sugar

2   beaten eggs

4 $\frac{1}{2}$ cups all-purpose flour

2   t. baking soda

2   t. cinnamon

2   t. ginger

$\frac{1}{4}$ t. salt

1 $\frac{1}{2}$ cups molasses

1 $\frac{1}{2}$ cups boiling water

Beat the eggs and sugar together well. Add the dry ingredients alternately with the melted butter or margarine and molasses. Beat well. Add the boiling water and mix completely. Pour into a well-oiled 9x13-in. pan and bake for approximately 1 hour at 350°.

Serves 16.

EPILOGUE–SERENDIPITY!

Webster says serendipity is "the faculty of finding valuable things not sought for," and on our Tripping Lightly adventures, we like to plan serendipitious touches for our fellow travelers. There's a contradiction here because one doesn't "plan" serendipity—it's just supposed to happen. In our case, however, we plan several serendipitious surprises for our guests. They're often food-related.

My favorite surprise takes place in Oregon in the Three Sisters Wilderness Area where we take a group backpacking for nine days each summer. On the final layover day before we hike out, we've been eating backpacking food for seven days, and our palates crave fresh food, or at least something that crunches besides sesame sticks and nuts. On this last day in the mountains, my co-guide and I take the group on a lovely hike to Moraine Lake where we insist they linger along the shoreline to memorize the mountains before we trek back to civilization.

Meanwhile back in town, and unannounced to the group, my co-guide's husband, Geoff, has loaded his backpack with a surprise meal for us including forty pounds of fruit, veggies, dips, french bread, crackers, cheese, smoked salmon, pasta salads, the makings of chocolate fondue, giant chocolate chip cookies, blueberries for morning pancakes, real maple syrup, and four liters of wine-in-a box! After he adds his personal gear, Geoff's pack weighs close to seventy-five pounds. He carries this load six miles uphill to the rendezvous, and when we return from our hike, there's Geoff. Picture us, sitting on the ground next to an alpine lake beside a creek, surrounded by mountains, as we sip white wine in our Sierra cups and feast on smoked salmon and crusty french bread. Now, there's serendipity!

It's hard to come up with anything so spectacular each time we travel but we try. When we make ice cream on a remote bank of the Oxbow part of the Snake River close to Grand Teton National Park, and watch the sun slip behind Mount Moran, we come close to Oregon's serendipity. When we spot a nearby moose and see its reflection in the Oxbow, it's a good show.

Wilderness travel is like that. Sometimes even the guides are surprised and sometimes we have to work harder to be clever. When we heat pecan bars inside the hood of the van while the engine is still hot and serve them a la mode at a campground, it evokes some oohs and aahs.

Extra touches bring unexpected elegance to camping. A fancy tablecloth, candles, a vase filled with fresh flowers, pumpkin carvings, and Mother's Day flowers all add serendipity to the experience for our groups. We turn squirt guns and rubber bands into toys, and set up primitive wilderness hair salons to keep ourselves lovely and fresh. We look for the fountain of eternal youth at hot springs, wherever we find them.

You see, primitive camping isn't about comfort deprivation and strenuous physical activity. Camping brings us to the woods so we can rediscover ourselves as joyful people who relish a good belly-laugh, delight in small pleasures, and remember how to to play.

ZEN VERSE

If you understand, things
are just as they are;
If you do not understand, things
are just as they are.